Understanding ReactJS: Building Modern Web Applications

In the ever-evolving landscape of web development, the quest for creating exceptional user experiences has led to the emergence of numerous frameworks and libraries. Among these, ReactJS stands tall as a game-changer, empowering developers to craft dynamic and responsive web applications with unparalleled ease and efficiency.

"Understanding ReactJS: Building Modern Web Applications" is a comprehensive guide that takes you on an exciting journey through the world of React. Whether you are a seasoned developer seeking to enhance your skill set or a newcomer eager to explore the realm of web development, this book is your roadmap to becoming a ReactJS virtuoso.

As the demand for interactive, fast, and user-friendly web applications continues to soar, ReactJS has become an indispensable tool for developers worldwide. With its component-based architecture, virtual DOM, and a vibrant community, React simplifies the creation of complex user interfaces and enables you to build applications that perform flawlessly across various devices and browsers.

This book delves deep into the framework's core concepts, best practices, and advanced techniques. From setting up your development environment to mastering state management, routing, and hooks, "Understanding ReactJS" offers a wealth of knowledge that will empower you to tackle real-world web development challenges.

What sets this book apart is its commitment to practicality. You'll find hands-on examples, code snippets, and real-world scenarios that guide you through the learning process. Whether you are developing a personal project, working on a startup, or contributing to a large-scale application, the insights shared within these pages will prove invaluable.

With ReactJS as your foundation and "Understanding ReactJS" as your guide, you'll be equipped to create modern web applications that not only meet but exceed user expectations. We invite you to embark on this journey of discovery, exploration, and mastery as you unlock the full potential of ReactJS.

Welcome to the world of "Understanding ReactJS: Building Modern Web Applications." Let's build something amazing together.

Happy coding!
Nikhil Ahir

Table of Contents

About This Book

Welcome to "Understanding ReactJS: Building Modern Web Applications." This book is your comprehensive guide to mastering the art of building web applications with ReactJS, one of the most popular and influential JavaScript libraries in the world of web development.

Who Is This Book For?

This book is designed for a diverse audience of developers, ranging from beginners looking to take their first steps in web development to experienced professionals seeking to enhance their knowledge of ReactJS. Whether you are a front-end developer, a full-stack engineer, or simply someone with a passion for creating web applications, this book has something valuable to offer you.

For beginners, we provide a gentle introduction to ReactJS, walking you through the fundamentals and gradually building your expertise. For more experienced developers, we dive deep into advanced topics and best practices, ensuring that you can build scalable and maintainable applications.

What Will You Learn?

In "ReactJS," you will embark on a journey that covers a wide range of topics, including:

- Understanding the core concepts of ReactJS and its component-based architecture.
- Creating responsive and interactive user interfaces with JSX and React components.
- Navigating your application with React Router.

- Managing state with Redux, a popular state management library.
- Harnessing the power of hooks to simplify component logic and code reuse.
- Building applications, from to-do lists to chat applications.
- Optimizing your application for performance and scalability.
- Implementing best practices and following coding standards.

Throughout this book, you will find practical examples, code snippets, and real-world projects that will help reinforce your understanding of ReactJS and its ecosystem.

How Is This Book Organized?

"ReactJS" is structured to guide you from the basics to advanced topics, ensuring a smooth learning curve:

- **Chapter 1: What Is ReactJS:** Provides an introduction to ReactJS, its core concepts, and key features.
- **Chapter 2: Getting Started with Components:** Covers the fundamentals of React components and how to create and use them.
- **Chapter 3: Building User Interfaces with React:** Explores rendering, conditional rendering, forms, and styling in React.
- **Chapter 4: React Router:** Focuses on navigation and routing in React applications.
- **Chapter 5: State Management with Redux:** Dives deep into state management using Redux.
- **Chapter 6: Hooks: Simplifying Component Logic:** Explores the use of hooks to manage state and side effects.
- **Chapter 7: Advanced Topics in React:** Covers error handling, portals, context API, testing, and more.
- **Chapter 8: Building Real-World Applications:** Walks you through the development of various real-world projects.
- **Chapter 9: Performance Optimization:** Discusses strategies for optimizing React applications.
- **Chapter 10: Best Practices and Tips:** Provides guidance on writing clean, maintainable, and performant code.
- **Appendices:** Include additional resources, a glossary, and an index.

How to Use This Book

To make the most of this book, we recommend reading it sequentially, starting with Chapter 1 and progressing through each chapter in order. Each chapter builds upon the knowledge gained in previous chapters, so a linear approach is ideal for beginners. Experienced developers may choose to jump to specific chapters of interest.

Feel free to experiment with the code examples provided, and don't hesitate to adapt them to your own projects. Learning by doing is a powerful approach, and we encourage you to apply the concepts you learn to your own web development endeavors.

We hope you find "ReactJS" to be a valuable resource on your journey to becoming a ReactJS expert. Let's begin this exciting journey together and unlock the full potential of ReactJS!

Acknowledgments

Writing a book is a journey that involves the contributions and support of many individuals, and I am deeply grateful to those who have played a significant role in making "Understanding ReactJS: Building Modern Web Applications" a reality.

First and foremost, I want to express my gratitude to the incredible ReactJS community and the open-source contributors who have dedicated their time and expertise to developing and maintaining React and its ecosystem. Your work has been instrumental in shaping this book.

To our families and friends, who have been unwavering in their support and understanding during the long hours and late nights of writing and research, thank you for your patience and encouragement. Your belief in us has been a constant source of motivation.

I extend my heartfelt appreciation to our technical reviewers and colleagues who provided invaluable feedback, insights, and suggestions that have enriched the content of this book. Your expertise and attention to detail have been instrumental in ensuring the accuracy and quality of the material.

Lastly, but certainly not least, I want to express my gratitude to you, the readers. Your interest in "ReactJS" is the reason I embarked on this journey. I hope this book provides you with valuable insights, skills, and inspiration to tackle your web development projects with confidence.

Thank you all for your contributions, support, and belief in this project. Together, we've created a resource that we hope will empower developers to master ReactJS and build modern web applications.

Sincerely,
Nikhil Ahir

Introduction to ReactJS

ReactJS

In the ever-evolving landscape of web development, ReactJS has emerged as a leading JavaScript library for building user interfaces. Before we dive into the details of how to use React effectively, let's start by understanding what ReactJS is and why it's become such a prominent tool in modern web development.

What Is ReactJS?

At its core, ReactJS, often simply referred to as React, is an open-source JavaScript library created by Facebook. It was first released in 2013 and has since gained immense popularity within the developer community. React is primarily used for building user interfaces (UIs) and single-page applications (SPAs).

The Component-Based Paradigm

One of the key concepts that sets React apart from other libraries and frameworks is its component-based architecture. In React, you break down your user interface into reusable building blocks called "components." Each component encapsulates a specific piece of the UI, complete with its own logic and rendering instructions.

For example, you might have components for a header, a navigation menu, a product card, or a login form. By composing your application from these modular components, you can create complex user interfaces that are easier to maintain, test, and scale.

Declarative and Virtual DOM

React embraces a declarative approach to building UIs. Instead of imperatively instructing the browser on how to update the DOM (Document Object Model) when data changes, you declare what the UI should look like based on the current application state. React then efficiently updates the DOM to match this desired state.

Under the hood, React employs a Virtual DOM (Document Object Model) to optimize this process. When data changes, React first updates a virtual representation of the DOM rather than directly manipulating the actual DOM elements. It then calculates the most efficient way to update the real DOM based on the changes in the virtual DOM. This approach results in improved performance and a more responsive user experience.

Key Features of ReactJS

ReactJS comes with a set of features that make it an attractive choice for building modern web applications:

- **Reusability:** The component-based architecture promotes code reusability and maintainability.
- **Virtual DOM:** The Virtual DOM enhances performance by minimizing unnecessary DOM updates.
- **One-way data flow:** React enforces a unidirectional data flow, making it easier to understand and debug your application.
- **Community and Ecosystem:** React has a vast and active community, with a rich ecosystem of libraries and tools.
- **Server-Side Rendering (SSR):** React can be used for server-side rendering, improving SEO and initial page load times.
- **Mobile App Development:** React Native, a framework built on top of React, allows you to build mobile apps for iOS and Android using the same React component structure.

In the following chapters, we'll delve deeper into these features and explore how to leverage them to build modern web applications.

Whether you're new to React or looking to deepen your understanding, this book will equip you with the knowledge and skills needed to master ReactJS.

The History of ReactJS

To truly understand the significance of ReactJS in the world of web development, it's essential to delve into its history and trace its origins. ReactJS, often referred to as React, was born out of the need for a more efficient way to build user interfaces for web applications, particularly within the vast and dynamic ecosystem of Facebook.

Inception at Facebook

ReactJS was developed by Jordan Walke, a software engineer at Facebook, and was first deployed on Facebook's newsfeed in 2011. The primary goal was to address the challenges Facebook faced in maintaining a performant and responsive user interface as the social media platform continued to grow in popularity.

Traditional approaches to web development involved manipulating the Document Object Model (DOM) directly to update the user interface in response to changes in data. This approach often led to inefficiencies and performance bottlenecks, especially in complex web applications.

React introduced a novel concept: the Virtual DOM. Instead of directly updating the real DOM, React maintained a lightweight, virtual representation of the DOM in memory. When changes occurred, React would compare this virtual representation to the real DOM and then calculate and apply the minimal set of updates needed to synchronize the two. This optimization dramatically improved performance by reducing unnecessary DOM manipulation.

Open-Source Release

In May 2013, Facebook officially open-sourced React, making it available to the wider developer community. This move marked a significant turning point in the history of web development. By releasing React as an open-source library, Facebook invited developers from around the world to contribute, collaborate, and leverage React in their own projects.

React quickly gained popularity, not just for its performance improvements but also for its declarative and component-based approach to building user interfaces. Developers found React to be a breath of fresh air in the often complex and fragmented landscape of front-end development.

React Ecosystem Growth

As React gained momentum, a thriving ecosystem of tools and libraries emerged around it. The React community actively contributed to the development of reusable components, state management solutions, routing libraries, and testing frameworks. This vibrant ecosystem further solidified React's position as a go-to choice for building modern web applications.

React Native: Expanding Beyond the Web

React's influence extended beyond web development when Facebook introduced React Native in 2015. React Native allowed developers to use React principles to build native mobile applications for both iOS and Android platforms. This move enabled code sharing between web and mobile applications, reducing development effort and accelerating cross-platform app development.

Continual Evolution

React has continued to evolve, introducing new features and improvements with each release. The React team at Facebook remains committed to the library's performance, developer experience, and backward compatibility. As a result, React has stood the test of time and remains a dominant force in the world of web development.

In this book, we will explore the core concepts and best practices of ReactJS, allowing you to harness the power of this influential library to build modern web applications. Whether you're a newcomer or a seasoned developer, understanding ReactJS is an invaluable skill that can propel your web development journey to new heights.

Key Features of ReactJS

ReactJS, commonly referred to as React, is renowned for its innovative approach to building user interfaces. Its popularity in the web development community can be attributed to a set of key features that distinguish it from other front-end libraries and frameworks. In this section, we'll explore these key features in more detail.

1. Component-Based Architecture

At the heart of React is its component-based architecture. In React, user interfaces are constructed using small, self-contained building blocks called components. Each component encapsulates a specific piece of the user interface, complete with its own logic and rendering instructions. This modular approach simplifies development, encourages code reusability, and enhances maintainability.

Think of a React component as a Lego block: you can create complex structures by combining these blocks. This concept aligns well with the principles of software engineering, making it easier to manage and scale applications, especially as they become more complex.

2. Declarative Syntax

React takes a declarative approach to building user interfaces. Instead of explicitly defining how to manipulate the Document Object Model (DOM) to reflect changes in data, you declare what the UI should look like based on the current application state. React takes care of updating the DOM efficiently to match this desired state.

This declarative syntax makes it easier to reason about your application's behavior and helps eliminate common sources of bugs that can occur in imperative code. You describe what you want, and React ensures that it happens.

3. Virtual DOM (Document Object Model)

React's Virtual DOM is a critical optimization that enhances performance. Rather than directly manipulating the real DOM, React maintains a lightweight, virtual representation of the DOM in memory. When data changes, React compares this virtual representation to the real DOM and calculates the most efficient way to update the real DOM.

This approach minimizes the number of actual DOM manipulations, resulting in faster updates and a more responsive user experience. The Virtual DOM is a key reason why React is known for its performance.

4. Reusable and Composable Components

React's component-based architecture encourages the creation of reusable and composable UI elements. You can build a library of components that can be used across different parts of your application or even in entirely separate projects. This reusability not only saves development time but also promotes consistency and a unified user experience.

5. Unidirectional Data Flow

React enforces a unidirectional data flow, meaning that data flows in a single direction within your application. This design pattern simplifies data management and reduces the likelihood of bugs related to data inconsistencies.

In a React application, data flows from parent components to child components, and child components can communicate changes to their parent components through callback functions. This clear and predictable data flow enhances the maintainability and understandability of your code.

6. Active Community and Ecosystem

React boasts a vast and active community of developers who continually contribute to its growth. This community has produced a rich ecosystem of open-source libraries, tools, and resources that enhance the development experience. Whether you need routing, state management, internationalization, or testing solutions, chances are there's a React library or package available to meet your needs.

7. Cross-Platform Development with React Native

While React is primarily associated with web development, React Native, a framework built on React principles, allows you to use the same component structure to build native mobile applications for iOS and Android. This approach enables code sharing between web and mobile applications, reducing development effort and accelerating cross-platform app development.

These key features make ReactJS a powerful and versatile library for building modern web applications. As you progress through this book, you'll gain a deeper understanding of how to harness these features to create interactive and performant user interfaces.

Setting Up Your Development Environment

Before we dive into the world of ReactJS and start building modern web applications, it's essential to set up your development environment. Having the right tools and configurations in place will make your journey smoother and more productive. In this section, we'll walk you through the steps to get your development environment ready for React development.

1. Node.js and npm

React development relies on Node.js, a JavaScript runtime that allows you to execute JavaScript on the server-side and manage dependencies with npm (Node Package Manager). If you don't already have Node.js installed, visit the official website (https://nodejs.org) to download and install the latest version for your platform. npm comes bundled with Node.js, so you don't need to install it separately.

To verify that Node.js and npm are correctly installed, open your terminal or command prompt and run the following commands:

bash
```
node -v
npm -v
```

These commands should display the versions of Node.js and npm you have installed. If you encounter any issues during installation or verification, consult the official documentation for guidance.

2. Code Editor

Choosing a code editor is a matter of personal preference, but we recommend using a code editor that supports JavaScript development efficiently. Some popular options include Visual Studio Code, Sublime

Text, Atom, and WebStorm. Visual Studio Code (VS Code) is a widely used and highly extensible code editor that offers excellent support for React development through extensions.

You can download VS Code from the official website (https://code.visualstudio.com) and explore the available extensions to enhance your React development experience.

3. Create React App

Create React App is an officially supported tool for quickly setting up a new React project with a predefined directory structure and build configuration. It simplifies the process of getting started with React and eliminates the need for complex build configurations.

To create a new React project using Create React App, open your terminal and run the following command:

bash
```
npx create-react-app my-react-app
```

Replace `my-react-app` with your preferred project name. This command will generate a new React project in a directory with the specified name. You can then navigate to the project directory:

bash
```
cd my-react-app
```

To start the development server and view your application in a web browser, run:

bash
```
npm start
```

This will launch the development server, and your React application will be accessible at `http://localhost:3000`.

4. Browser Developer Tools

A web browser is an essential tool for web development. Modern browsers come with built-in developer tools that allow you to inspect and debug your web applications. While you can use any browser, Google Chrome is known for its excellent developer tools and extensive debugging capabilities. Ensure that your preferred browser is up to date and familiarize yourself with its developer tools.

With these tools in place, you're ready to start your journey into React development. In the chapters that follow, we'll explore React's core concepts, best practices, and advanced techniques, helping you build modern web applications with confidence.

Your First React Component

Now that your development environment is set up, it's time to dive into React by creating your first React component. In React, everything revolves around components, which are the building blocks of your user interface. Components can be as simple as a button or as complex as an entire webpage.

In this section, we'll guide you through the process of creating a basic React component and rendering it on a web page. By the end of this section, you'll have a solid understanding of how React components work.

Creating a React App

As mentioned earlier, Create React App simplifies the process of setting up a new React project. Please follow the steps mentioned in chapter **Setting Up Your Development Environment** to create a react app.

Creating Your First Component

Now that you have a React app set up, let's create your first React component. Open your code editor (e.g., Visual Studio Code) and navigate to the `src` directory of your React app. Inside the `src` directory, you'll find a file called `App.js`. This is the entry point to your React application.

Open `App.js` and replace its contents with the following code:

jsx

```
import React from 'react';

function App() {
  return (
    <div>
      <h1>Hello, React!</h1>
      <p>This is your first React component.</p>
    </div>
  );
}

export default App;
```

In this code:

- We import the `React` module, which is required for working with React components.
- We define a functional component named `App`. This component returns JSX (JavaScript XML), which describes the structure of our user interface.
- Inside the `return` statement, we have a `div` element containing an `h1` (header) element and a `p` (paragraph) element. These are standard HTML elements, but notice how they are written in JSX within the JavaScript code.

Rendering Your Component

Now that you've created your `App` component, it's time to render it on the web page. Open the `src/index.js` file in your code editor and replace its contents with the following code:

jsx

```jsx
import React from 'react';
import ReactDOM from 'react-dom';
import App from './App';

ReactDOM.render(
  <React.StrictMode>
    <App />
  </React.StrictMode>,
  document.getElementById('root')
);
```

Here's what's happening in this code:

- We import the necessary modules, including `React`, `ReactDOM`, and the `App` component we created.
- We use `ReactDOM.render` to render the `App` component into the HTML element with the id of `root`. This is where your React application will appear on the web page.

Viewing Your React App

To see your React app in action, follow these steps:

1. Make sure you're in the root directory of your React app in your terminal.

2. Start the development server by running:

bash

```bash
npm start
```

3. Open your web browser and navigate to `http://localhost:3000`. You should see your React app displaying "Hello, React!" and "This is your first React component."

Congratulations! You've just created and rendered your first React component. This is just the beginning of your journey into React development. In the chapters that follow, we'll explore React's concepts and features in greater depth, allowing you to build increasingly complex and interactive web applications.

Getting Started with Components

Understanding Components

Components are at the core of React development. They are the building blocks of your user interface, allowing you to encapsulate and manage the different parts of your application. In this chapter, we'll dive deeper into understanding what components are and how they work in React.

What Are Components?

In React, a component is a self-contained, reusable piece of user interface that can be as simple as a button or as complex as an entire webpage. Components are the fundamental units of your application, and you can think of them as custom HTML elements. They encapsulate both the visual elements (what you see) and the behavior (how it works) of a part of your application.

The power of components lies in their ability to be composed together to create complex user interfaces. You can build a library of components that represent various parts of your application, and then reuse them across different parts of your project. This modularity not only simplifies development but also promotes consistency and maintainability.

Types of Components

React supports two primary types of components:

1. **Functional Components:** Functional components are JavaScript functions that take in properties (props) as input and return JSX elements as output. They are also known as "stateless" components

because they don't manage their own internal state. Functional components are simple, easy to read, and are the recommended choice for building presentational or UI-focused components.

jsx
```jsx
function MyComponent(props) {
   return <div>Hello, {props.name}!</div>;
}
```

2. Class Components: Class components are JavaScript classes that extend the `React.Component` class. They have their own internal state and lifecycle methods, making them suitable for managing complex component behavior, side effects, and state.

jsx
```jsx
class MyComponent extends React.Component {
   constructor(props) {
      super(props);
      this.state = { count: 0 };
   }

   render() {
     return (
       <div>
          Count: {this.state.count}
          <button onClick={() =>
this.setState({ count: this.state.count + 1 })}>
             Increment
          </button>
       </div>
     );
   }
}
```

Props: Input to Components

Props, short for "properties," are a fundamental concept in React. They allow you to pass data from a parent component to a child component. Props are read-only and help you make your components reusable by configuring their behavior based on external data.

In functional components, props are passed as arguments to the component function. In class components, props are accessed using `this.props`.

Here's an example of passing and using props in a functional component:

jsx
```jsx
function Welcome(props) {
  return <h1>Hello, {props.name}</h1>;
}

const element = <Welcome name="Alice" />;
```

In this example, the `Welcome` component receives the `name` prop and displays it within an `<h1>` element.

State: Managing Component Data

While props allow you to pass data into a component, state is used to manage data that can change over time and affect a component's behavior and rendering. Class components can have their own state, which can be initialized in the constructor and updated using the `setState` method.

Here's an example of a class component with state:

jsx
```jsx
class Counter extends React.Component {
```

```
  constructor(props) {
    super(props);
    this.state = { count: 0 };
  }

  render() {
    return (
      <div>
        Count: {this.state.count}
        <button onClick={() => this.setState({
count: this.state.count + 1 })}>
          Increment
        </button>
      </div>
    );
  }
}
```

In this example, the `Counter` component manages a `count` state variable that is initially set to 0 and can be incremented when the button is clicked.

Understanding components, props, and state is foundational to React development. These concepts enable you to build modular, reusable, and dynamic user interfaces. As you progress through this book, you'll explore more advanced techniques and best practices for working with components and creating interactive web applications.

Functional Components

Functional components are one of the fundamental building blocks of React applications. They are JavaScript functions that take in properties (props) as input and return JSX elements as output. Functional components are also known as "stateless" components because they don't manage their own internal state. Here, we'll explore functional components in greater detail and see how to create and use them effectively.

Creating a Functional Component

Creating a functional component is straightforward. You define a JavaScript function that accepts props as its argument and returns JSX elements. Let's create a simple functional component that displays a welcome message:

```jsx
// Functional component
function Welcome(props) {
  return <h1>Hello, {props.name}!</h1>;
}
```

In this example:

- We define a function named `Welcome` that takes a `props` argument.
- Inside the function, we use JSX to define the structure of the component, including an `<h1>` element that displays a welcome message.

Using a Functional Component

Once you've created a functional component, you can use it just like any other HTML element in your JSX. To use the `Welcome` component we defined earlier, you can do the following:

jsx
```
// Using the Welcome component
const element = <Welcome name="Alice" />;
```

In this code, we create an instance of the `Welcome` component and pass a `name` prop with the value "Alice." This instance of the component can now be included in your JSX to render the welcome message.

jsx
```
// Rendering the Welcome component
ReactDOM.render(element,
document.getElementById('root'));
```

In this example, we use `ReactDOM.render` to render the `element` (which is an instance of the `Welcome` component) into the HTML element with the id of `'root'`.

Props in Functional Components

Props are a crucial part of functional components. They allow you to pass data from a parent component to a child component, making your components dynamic and reusable. In the `Welcome` component we created earlier, the `name` prop is used to customize the message displayed.

jsx
```jsx
// Using props in a functional component
function Welcome(props) {
  return <h1>Hello, {props.name}!</h1>;
}

const element = <Welcome name="Alice" />;
```

In this code, the `name` prop is passed to the `Welcome` component, and within the component, it is accessed using `props.name`. This allows you to create instances of the `Welcome` component with different names.

Functional Components and Reusability

One of the strengths of functional components is their reusability. You can create simple, self-contained components and reuse them throughout your application. For example, you could use the `Welcome` component to display greetings in various parts of your user interface.

jsx
```jsx
const greeting1 = <Welcome name="Alice" />;
const greeting2 = <Welcome name="Bob" />;
const greeting3 = <Welcome name="Charlie" />;
```

In this code, we create multiple instances of the `Welcome` component to greet different users.

Functional components are a fundamental building block in React development. They are especially useful for creating presentational or UI-focused components that primarily render content based on the props they receive. In the next sections, we'll explore class components, which provide more advanced features, such as managing internal state and lifecycle methods, for handling complex behavior in your applications.

Class Components

In addition to functional components, React also allows you to create class components. Class components are JavaScript classes that extend the `React.Component` class. They provide a way to manage component-specific state, handle lifecycle methods, and encapsulate complex behavior. Class components have been a core part of React for many years and are still widely used, although functional components with hooks have become increasingly popular.

Creating a Class Component

To create a class component in React, you define a JavaScript class that extends `React.Component` and implement a `render` method. The `render` method returns JSX, defining the structure and appearance of the component. Here's a simple example of a class component:

jsx
```
// Class component
class Greeting extends React.Component {
   render() {
     return <h1>Hello, React!</h1>;
   }
}
```

In this example:

- We define a class called `Greeting` that extends `React.Component`.
- Inside the class, we implement a `render` method that returns JSX to define the component's appearance.

Using a Class Component

Once you've created a class component, you can use it just like functional components. You can create an instance of the class component and include it in your JSX. Here's how you can use the `Greeting` class component:

jsx
```
// Using the Greeting class component
const element = <Greeting />;
```

In this code, we create an instance of the `Greeting` class component and store it in the `element` variable. This instance can then be included in your JSX to render the greeting.

jsx
```
// Rendering the Greeting component
ReactDOM.render(element,
document.getElementById('root'));
```

In this example, we use `ReactDOM.render` to render the `element` (which is an instance of the `Greeting` component) into the HTML element with the id of `'root'`.

State in Class Components

One of the key features of class components is their ability to manage state. State allows components to store and manage data that can change over time. To use state in a class component, you initialize it in the component's constructor and access it using `this.state`. You can also update state using `this.setState`.

Here's an example of a class component that manages a `count` state variable:

jsx
```
// Class component with state
class Counter extends React.Component {
  constructor(props) {
    super(props);
    this.state = { count: 0 };
  }

  render() {
    return (
      <div>
        Count: {this.state.count}
        <button onClick={() => this.setState({
count: this.state.count + 1 })}>
          Increment
        </button>
      </div>
    );
  }
}
```

In this code:

- We define a `Counter` class component that initializes a `count` state variable in the constructor.
- In the `render` method, we display the current count and provide a button to increment it.
- When the button is clicked, we use `this.setState` to update the `count` state.

Lifecycle Methods

Class components also provide lifecycle methods that allow you to hook into various stages of a component's lifecycle, such as when it's created, updated, or unmounted. These lifecycle methods can be used for tasks like data fetching, setting up subscriptions, or cleaning up resources.

Here are some common lifecycle methods in class components:

- **componentDidMount:** Called after the component is inserted into the DOM.
- **componentDidUpdate:** Called after the component's props or state change and after the component is re-rendered.
- **componentWillUnmount:** Called before the component is removed from the DOM.

Lifecycle methods are powerful but are less commonly used in modern React development due to the introduction of hooks, which provide a more flexible and composable way to manage component behavior.

Class components are still relevant in React and can be particularly useful when you need to manage complex state or utilize lifecycle methods. However, as you continue your journey into React development, you'll find that functional components with hooks offer a more concise and modern approach to building components and managing behavior. In the next sections, we'll explore hooks and how they can be used in both functional and class components.

JSX: JavaScript XML

In React, JSX (JavaScript XML) is a syntax extension that allows you to write HTML-like code within your JavaScript or TypeScript files. JSX makes it easier to define the structure and appearance of your components. It is a fundamental part of React development and plays a crucial role in creating user interfaces.

Why Use JSX?

JSX has several advantages that make it a powerful choice for defining user interfaces in React:

1. **Readability:** JSX code resembles HTML, making it easy to read and understand. This readability is especially valuable when working with complex user interfaces.

2. **Component Composition:** JSX allows you to create and compose custom components just like HTML elements. You can use components you've created or ones provided by third-party libraries seamlessly within JSX.

3. **Expressiveness:** JSX supports embedding JavaScript expressions within curly braces `{}`. This allows you to inject dynamic data, compute values, and execute functions directly within your JSX code.

4. **Tooling Support:** JSX is widely supported by development tools and editors. Most code editors provide syntax highlighting, auto-completion, and error checking for JSX code.

JSX Basics

Here are some fundamental aspects of JSX:

- **Elements:** JSX allows you to define elements that represent parts of your user interface. Elements can be HTML elements like `<div>`, React components, or user-defined components.

jsx
```jsx
const element = <div>Hello, React!</div>;
```

- **Attributes:** You can set attributes on JSX elements just like in HTML. Attribute values can be static strings or JavaScript expressions enclosed in curly braces.

jsx
```jsx
const title = 'Welcome to React';
const element = <h1 title={title}>Hello,
React!</h1>;
```

- **Embedding Expressions:** You can embed JavaScript expressions within curly braces `{}` in JSX. These expressions are evaluated and their results are inserted into the JSX element.

jsx
```jsx
const name = 'Alice';
const element = <p>Hello, {name}!</p>;
```

- **Self-Closing Tags:** For elements without children, you can use self-closing tags, just like in HTML.

jsx
```jsx
const image = <img src="example.jpg" alt="Example" />;
```

- **Comments:** You can add comments within JSX using curly braces `{/* */}`.

jsx

```
const element = (
  <div>
    <p>Hello, React!</p>
    {/* This is a JSX comment */}
  </div>
);
```

- **Multiple Elements:** JSX can only have a single root element. If you want to render multiple elements, you can wrap them in a parent container.

jsx
```
const elements = (
  <div>
    <p>Element 1</p>
    <p>Element 2</p>
  </div>
);
```

JSX and Babel

JSX is not natively understood by browsers. To make JSX code compatible with browsers, it needs to be transpiled into regular JavaScript. Babel, a popular JavaScript compiler, is commonly used for this purpose. Babel can convert JSX code into JavaScript that can be executed in browsers.

When you set up a React project using tools like Create React App, Babel is configured to transpile JSX code for you, allowing you to write JSX without worrying about the underlying conversion.

Here's an example of JSX code:

jsx
```
const element = <h1>Hello, React!</h1>;
```

And here's the equivalent JavaScript code after transpilation:

javascript
```
const element = React.createElement("h1", null,
"Hello, React!");
```

While you can write React applications without JSX by directly using
`React.createElement`, JSX greatly improves code readability and
maintainability.

Understanding JSX is essential for React development, as it serves as the
primary way to define your component's structure and appearance. As
you continue your journey into React, you'll become more comfortable
and proficient in using JSX to create dynamic and interactive user
interfaces.

Props: Properties for Components

Props, short for "properties," are a fundamental concept in React. They allow you to pass data from a parent component to a child component. Props are read-only and provide a way to configure and customize the behavior and appearance of components. In this section, we'll explore props in greater detail and see how to use them effectively.

Passing Props

In React, props are passed from parent components to child components. This mechanism allows you to share data and behavior between components and create dynamic and reusable user interfaces.

Here's how you can pass props from a parent component to a child component:

1. Define the parent component, which includes the child component in its JSX. Pass the desired data or values as attributes to the child component.

jsx
```
// Parent component
function App() {
  return <Greeting name="Alice" />;
}
```

In this example, the `name` prop is passed to the `Greeting` component.

2. Access the props in the child component by defining them as arguments in the component function or by accessing them using `this.props` in class components.

jsx

```
// Child component
function Greeting(props) {
  return <h1>Hello, {props.name}!</h1>;
}
```

In the `Greeting` component, we access the `name` prop using `props.name` within the JSX.

Using Props in Functional Components

In functional components, you can access props directly as function arguments. Here's an example of how you can use props in a functional component:

jsx
```
function Welcome(props) {
  return <h1>Hello, {props.name}!</h1>;
}
```

In this code, the `Welcome` component receives a `name` prop and displays it within an `<h1>` element.

Using Props in Class Components

In class components, you can access props using `this.props`. Here's how you can use props in a class component:

jsx
```
class Welcome extends React.Component {
  render() {
    return <h1>Hello, {this.props.name}!</h1>;
  }
}
```

In this example, the `Welcome` class component accesses the `name` prop using `this.props.name` within the `render` method.

Default Props

You can also specify default values for props using the `defaultProps` property. This allows you to provide fallback values for props that are not explicitly passed from the parent component.

Here's an example of setting default props for a functional component:

jsx
```
function Greeting(props) {
   return <h1>Hello, {props.name}!</h1>;
}

Greeting.defaultProps = {
   name: 'Guest',
};
```

In this code, if the `name` prop is not provided when using the `Greeting` component, it will default to "Guest."

Props Validation

React provides a way to validate the props that a component receives using the `propTypes` property. While this is not required, it can help catch errors and bugs early in development.

Here's an example of defining prop types for a functional component:

jsx

```
import PropTypes from 'prop-types';

function Greeting(props) {
  return <h1>Hello, {props.name}!</h1>;
}

Greeting.propTypes = {
  name: PropTypes.string.isRequired,
};
```

In this code, we use the `PropTypes` library to define the `name` prop as a required string. If a component using `Greeting` doesn't provide the `name` prop or provides a non-string value, a warning will be displayed in the browser's console during development.

Props are a powerful mechanism in React for passing data between components and configuring their behavior. They make it possible to create reusable and composable components, which is a key principle in React development. As you build more complex applications, you'll find props to be an essential tool for creating dynamic and interactive user interfaces.

State and Lifecycle

In React, components can have both `props` and `state`. While `props` are used for passing data from parent components to child components, `state` is used for managing data that can change over time and affect a component's behavior and rendering. Understanding how to work with `state` and the component lifecycle is essential for building dynamic and interactive user interfaces.

State in React Components

State is an internal data storage mechanism that allows components to store and manage data that can change. Unlike `props`, which are passed down from parent components and considered read-only, `state` is mutable and can be updated within a component.

To add `state` to a class component, you need to do the following:

1. Initialize state in the constructor by setting `this.state` to an object with the initial values of your state variables.

jsx
```
class Counter extends React.Component {
  constructor(props) {
    super(props);
    this.state = { count: 0 };
  }
}
```

In this example, we initialize the `count` state variable to 0.

2. Access and update state using `this.state` and `this.setState`. You should never modify `state` directly.

jsx

```
class Counter extends React.Component {
  constructor(props) {
    super(props);
    this.state = { count: 0 };
  }

  increment() {
    this.setState({ count: this.state.count + 1
});
  }
}
```

In this code, the `increment` method is used to update the `count` state.

Rendering State Data

Once you have state data in a component, you can render it in your component's JSX using curly braces `{}`.

jsx
```
class Counter extends React.Component {
  constructor(props) {
    super(props);
    this.state = { count: 0 };
  }

  render() {
    return (
      <div>
        Count: {this.state.count}
        <button onClick={() =>
this.increment()}>Increment</button>
      </div>
    );
  }
}
```

In this example, we render the current value of `count` within the JSX, making it visible to the user.

Updating State

To update state in React components, you should always use the `this.setState` method. It takes an object as an argument, where each key corresponds to a state variable you want to update. React will merge the changes into the existing state.

jsx
```
class Counter extends React.Component {
  constructor(props) {
    super(props);
    this.state = { count: 0 };
  }

  increment() {
    this.setState({ count: this.state.count + 1 });
  }
}
```

In this code, the `increment` method updates the `count` state by incrementing its value by 1. React will automatically re-render the component with the updated state, reflecting the changes in the user interface.

Component Lifecycle

React components have a lifecycle that consists of various phases, such as mounting, updating, and unmounting. Each phase provides hooks or methods that you can use to perform actions at specific points in the component's life.

Here are some common lifecycle methods in class components:

- **componentDidMount:** Called after the component is inserted into the DOM. It's a good place to initiate data fetching, set up subscriptions, or perform one-time setup.

- **componentDidUpdate:** Called after the component's props or state change and after the component is re-rendered. It's useful for responding to changes in the component's data.

- **componentWillUnmount:** Called before the component is removed from the DOM. It's a good place to clean up resources like event listeners or timers.

For example, you can use `componentDidMount` to fetch data from an API when the component is first rendered, and `componentWillUnmount` to clean up any resources or subscriptions when the component is removed from the DOM.

jsx
```jsx
class MyComponent extends React.Component {
  componentDidMount() {
    // Fetch data from an API when the component is
first mounted
    fetchData().then((data) => {
      this.setState({ data });
    });
  }

  componentWillUnmount() {
    // Clean up any resources or subscriptions when
the component is unmounted
    cleanupResources();
  }
}
```

Understanding the component lifecycle and when to use lifecycle methods is crucial for managing complex behavior and side effects in your components.

State and Lifecycle Summary

In summary, `state` and the component lifecycle are fundamental concepts in React development:

- `state` allows components to manage and update data that can change over time.
- You should never modify `state` directly; always use `this.setState` to update it.
- The component lifecycle provides hooks and methods that allow you to perform actions at specific points in a component's life, such as fetching data or cleaning up resources.

As you continue your journey into React development, you'll find that state and the component lifecycle are essential tools for creating dynamic and interactive user interfaces.

Component Lifecycle Methods

In React, class components have a lifecycle that consists of various phases or stages. These phases provide developers with hooks or methods that allow you to perform actions at specific points in a component's life. Understanding the component lifecycle is crucial for managing component behavior, side effects, and interactions with the DOM.

Here are some of the most commonly used lifecycle methods in React class components:

1. **constructor(props):** This is the constructor for your component, and it's called when an instance of the component is created. You can use it to initialize state and bind methods. Be sure to call `super(props)` as the first statement in your constructor if you're extending `React.Component`.

jsx
```
constructor(props) {
  super(props);
  this.state = { count: 0 };
}
```

2. **render():** The `render` method is responsible for rendering the component's output. It should return JSX that defines the component's structure and appearance. This method is called whenever the component's state or props change.

jsx
```
render() {
  return <div>Count: {this.state.count}</div>;
}
```

3. **componentDidMount():** This method is called after the component is inserted into the DOM. It's a good place to initiate data fetching, set up

subscriptions, or perform one-time setup. It's commonly used for tasks that need to happen once the component is fully rendered and visible.

jsx
```jsx
componentDidMount() {
  fetchData().then((data) => {
    this.setState({ data });
  });
}
```

4. componentDidUpdate(prevProps, prevState): This method is called after the component's props or state change and after the component is re-rendered. It's useful for responding to changes in the component's data. You can compare the previous props and state with the current ones to determine how they've changed.

jsx
```jsx
componentDidUpdate(prevProps, prevState) {
    if (this.props.userID !== prevProps.userID) {
      // Perform some action when the userID prop
changes
    }
}
```

5. componentWillUnmount(): This method is called before the component is removed from the DOM. It's a good place to clean up resources like event listeners or timers to prevent memory leaks.

jsx
```jsx
componentWillUnmount() {
  cleanupResources();
}
```

These are some of the most commonly used lifecycle methods in React class components. Keep in mind that React has additional lifecycle methods that you can use for more specific scenarios.

It's important to note that with the introduction of React Hooks, functional components can also manage component lifecycle behavior using hooks like useEffect. Hooks provide a more flexible and composable way to achieve the same functionality as class component lifecycle methods.

Understanding the component lifecycle is valuable when working with class components, but as you explore more modern React development, you may find that functional components with hooks offer a more concise and expressive way to manage component behavior.

Building User Interfaces with React

Working with JSX

In React, JSX (JavaScript XML) is the primary syntax for defining the structure and appearance of your user interfaces. JSX is a powerful and expressive extension to JavaScript that allows you to write HTML-like code within your JavaScript files. It simplifies the process of creating and rendering user interfaces in a way that is both familiar and efficient.

JSX Syntax

JSX syntax resembles HTML, making it easy to read and write. It allows you to define elements, attributes, and components using a familiar syntax. Here are some key points about JSX syntax:

- **Elements:** JSX allows you to create elements that represent parts of your user interface. Elements can be HTML elements like <div> or React components.

```jsx
const element = <div>Hello, React!</div>;
```

- **Attributes:** Just like in HTML, you can set attributes on JSX elements using the same syntax.

```jsx
const element = <img src="example.jpg" alt="Example" />;
```

- **Embedding Expressions:** You can embed JavaScript expressions within curly braces {} in JSX. These expressions are evaluated and their results are inserted into the JSX element.

jsx
```
const name = 'Alice';
const element = <p>Hello, {name}!</p>;
```

- **Self-Closing Tags:** For elements without children, you can use self-closing tags, similar to HTML.

jsx
```
const element = <input type="text" />;
```

- **Comments:** You can add comments within JSX using curly braces `{/* */}`.

jsx
```
const element = (
  <div>
    <p>Hello, React!</p>
    {/* This is a JSX comment */}
  </div>
);
```

Embedding JavaScript Expressions

One of the powerful features of JSX is the ability to embed JavaScript expressions within curly braces `{}`. This allows you to inject dynamic data, compute values, and execute functions directly within your JSX code. Here's an example:

jsx

```
const name = 'Alice';
const element = <p>Hello, {name}!</p>;
```

In this code, the name variable is embedded within the JSX using {name}. The value of name will be dynamically inserted into the rendered output.

JSX and Babel

JSX code is not natively understood by browsers. To make JSX code compatible with browsers, it needs to be transpiled into regular JavaScript. Babel, a popular JavaScript compiler, is commonly used for this purpose. Babel can convert JSX code into JavaScript that can be executed in browsers.

Here's an example of JSX code:

jsx
```
const element = <h1>Hello, React!</h1>;
```

After transpilation, it looks like this:

javascript
```
const element = React.createElement("h1", null,
"Hello, React!");
```

While you can write React applications without JSX by directly using React.createElement, JSX greatly improves code readability and maintainability.

Summary

JSX is a fundamental part of React development. It simplifies the process of defining the structure and appearance of your user interfaces, making it easier to create dynamic and interactive web applications. As you continue working with React, you'll become more proficient in using JSX to build complex user interfaces and harness the power of JavaScript within your components.

Creating and Rendering Elements

In React, creating and rendering elements is a fundamental concept. Elements are the building blocks of your user interfaces, representing the structure and content of your application. React provides a straightforward way to create elements and render them to the DOM.

Creating Elements

In React, elements are created using JSX syntax. Elements can represent both built-in HTML elements (like <div>, <p>, or <img>) and custom React components.

To create an element, you simply write JSX code that describes what you want the element to look like. Here are some examples:

```jsx
const heading = <h1>Hello, React!</h1>;
const paragraph = <p>This is a React paragraph.</p>;
const image = <img src="example.jpg" alt="Example" />;
```

In these examples, we've created elements for a heading, a paragraph, and an image using JSX. These elements can then be rendered to the DOM.

Rendering Elements

Once you've created elements, you need to render them to the DOM to make them visible to the user. React provides the ReactDOM.render() method for this purpose. You specify the element you want to render and the target DOM element where it should be placed.

Here's an example of rendering an element:

jsx
```
const element = <h1>Hello, React!</h1>;
ReactDOM.render(element,
document.getElementById('root'));
```

In this code, we create an element representing an <h1> heading, and then we use ReactDOM.render() to render it into the HTML element with the id of **root**. As a result, the "Hello, React!" heading will be displayed in the web page where the **root** element is located.

Updating Elements

In React, elements are not mutable. Once an element is created and rendered, you can't change its content or attributes directly. Instead, you create a new element with the desired changes and re-render it. React will efficiently update the DOM to reflect the changes.

Here's an example of updating an element's content:

jsx
```
const element = <h1>Hello, React!</h1>;
ReactDOM.render(element,
document.getElementById('root'));

// Later, update the element
const updatedElement = <h1>Hello, Updated
React!</h1>;
ReactDOM.render(updatedElement,
document.getElementById('root'));
```

In this code, we first render the initial element with the text "Hello, React!" into the DOM. Later, we create a new updatedElement with the text "Hello, Updated React!" and re-render it into the same DOM element. React efficiently updates the content, and the user sees the updated text.

Summary

Creating and rendering elements is a fundamental concept in React. Elements represent the structure and content of your user interfaces, and you create them using JSX syntax. Once created, elements can be rendered to the DOM using ReactDOM.render(). To update elements, you create new elements with the desired changes and re-render them, allowing React to efficiently update the DOM.

As you continue working with React, you'll build more complex user interfaces by creating and rendering elements, and you'll discover how React's component-based architecture enables the construction of dynamic and interactive applications.

Conditional Rendering

Conditional rendering is a crucial concept in React that allows you to conditionally display different content or components based on certain conditions or user interactions. React provides several ways to achieve conditional rendering, allowing you to create dynamic and responsive user interfaces.

Using the if Statement

One of the simplest ways to implement conditional rendering in React is by using JavaScript's `if` statement within your component's render method. You can conditionally determine what JSX to return based on the evaluation of a condition.

Here's an example of conditional rendering using an if statement:

jsx
```
class Greeting extends React.Component {
  render() {
    if (this.props.isLoggedIn) {
      return <h1>Welcome back, User!</h1>;
    } else {
      return <h1>Please log in</h1>;
    }
  }
}
```

In this code, the Greeting component checks the isLoggedIn prop and renders different content based on whether the user is logged in or not.

Using Ternary Operator

A more concise way to achieve conditional rendering is by using the ternary operator (`condition ? true : false`) within JSX. It allows you to conditionally render content in a single expression.

Here's an example using the ternary operator for conditional rendering:

jsx
```
class Greeting extends React.Component {
  render() {
    return (
      <div>
        {this.props.isLoggedIn ? (
          <h1>Welcome back, User!</h1>
        ) : (
          <h1>Please log in</h1>
        )}
      </div>
    );
  }
}
```

In this code, the ternary operator is used to determine whether to display the "Welcome back, User!" message or the "Please log in" message based on the `isLoggedIn` prop.

Using Logical && Operator

Another concise way to conditionally render elements is by using the logical `&&` operator within JSX. You can conditionally render an element if a certain condition is met, and if not, you can render null or false, effectively rendering nothing.

Here's an example using the `&&` operator for conditional rendering:

jsx

```
class Greeting extends React.Component {
  render() {
    return (
      <div>
        {this.props.isLoggedIn && <h1>Welcome back,
User!</h1>}
      </div>
    );
  }
}
```

In this code, the <h1> element is rendered only if this.props.isLoggedIn is true. If it's false, nothing is rendered.

Using if-else Statements

For more complex conditional rendering logic, you can use `if-else` statements or switch statements within your render method. This approach allows you to handle multiple conditions and render different content accordingly.

jsx
```
class Greeting extends React.Component {
  render() {
    let message;
    if (this.props.isLoggedIn) {
      message = <h1>Welcome back, User!</h1>;
    } else if (this.props.isRegistered) {
      message = <h1>Please log in</h1>;
    } else {
      message = <h1>Please sign up</h1>;
    }
    return <div>{message}</div>;
  }
}
```

In this example, the Greeting component evaluates multiple conditions and assigns the appropriate message to the message variable, which is then rendered in the JSX.

Summary

Conditional rendering is a powerful feature in React that allows you to create dynamic user interfaces that respond to user interactions and changing data. You can achieve conditional rendering using if statements, the ternary operator, the && operator, or if-else statements, depending on the complexity of your conditions.

By mastering conditional rendering, you can create user interfaces that adapt and provide a personalized experience to your users, enhancing the overall usability of your React applications.

Lists and Keys

In many web applications, you'll need to display lists of items, such as user-generated content, search results, or product listings. React provides a convenient way to work with lists by allowing you to map over arrays and render a component for each item. Additionally, React requires you to use keys to help it efficiently update and identify individual list items.

Creating Lists

To create a list in React, you map over an array of data and render a component for each item. Here's an example of how to create a simple list of items:

```jsx
class ItemList extends React.Component {
  render() {
    const items = this.props.items;
    const itemElements = items.map((item) => <li
key={item.id}>{item.name}</li>);

    return <ul>{itemElements}</ul>;
  }
}
```

In this code, the `ItemList` component receives an array of `items` as a prop. It then uses the `map` function to create a new array of `itemElements`, where each item in the array is represented by a `<li>` element. The `key` prop is used to uniquely identify each list item.

Using Keys

Keys are important in React when rendering lists. They help React identify which items have changed, been added, or been removed. It's essential that each key is unique within the list and remains consistent across re-renders. In the example above, we used `item.id` as the key, assuming that `item.id` is unique for each item.

React uses keys to optimize list rendering and update performance. Without keys, React may have to re-render the entire list when items change, which can be inefficient. With keys, React can identify which specific items have changed and update only those items in the DOM.

Dynamic Lists

Lists in React can be dynamic, which means they can change over time based on user interactions or data updates. You can re-render the list whenever the underlying data changes. Here's an example:

jsx
```
class DynamicList extends React.Component {
  constructor(props) {
    super(props);
    this.state = { items: this.props.initialItems };
  }

  addItem = () => {
    const newItem = { id: Date.now(), name: 'New
Item' };
    this.setState({ items: [...this.state.items,
newItem] });
  };

  render() {
    const items = this.state.items;
```

```
    const itemElements = items.map((item) => <li
key={item.id}>{item.name}</li>);

    return (
      <div>
        <button onClick={this.addItem}>Add
Item</button>
        <ul>{itemElements}</ul>
      </div>
    );
  }
}
```

In this code, the `DynamicList` component starts with an initial set of items. When the "Add Item" button is clicked, a new item is added to the list, and the component re-renders with the updated list.

Summary

Working with lists and keys is a fundamental aspect of building user interfaces with React. React's ability to efficiently update and manage lists based on changes in data or user interactions makes it a powerful tool for building dynamic and responsive web applications. By understanding how to create lists, use keys effectively, and handle dynamic lists, you'll be well-equipped to work with lists of data in your React applications.

Styling in React

Styling is an essential part of creating visually appealing and user-friendly web applications. React provides various approaches for styling your components and user interfaces. In this section, we'll explore different ways to style React components.

Inline Styles

One of the simplest ways to style React components is by using inline styles. Inline styles allow you to define styles directly within your JSX using JavaScript objects. This approach can be useful for applying styles conditionally or dynamically based on props or state.

Here's an example of using inline styles in a React component:

jsx
```jsx
class StyledComponent extends React.Component {
  render() {
    const style = {
      backgroundColor: 'lightblue',
      padding: '10px',
      border: '1px solid #ccc',
    };

    return <div style={style}>Styled
Component</div>;
  }
}
```

In this code, we define a `style` object and apply it to the `div` element using the `style` prop. The styles are specified as key-value pairs within the object.

CSS Stylesheets

Another common way to style React components is by using CSS stylesheets. You can create separate `.css` files for your styles and import them into your React components. This approach provides a clean separation of concerns between your styling and component logic.

Here's an example of using a CSS stylesheet in a React component:

jsx
```
import './StyledComponent.css';

class StyledComponent extends React.Component {
  render() {
    return <div className="styled-component">Styled
Component</div>;
  }
}
```

In this code, we import a CSS file named `StyledComponent.css` and apply the styles to the `div` element using the `className` prop.

CSS-in-JS Libraries

For more dynamic and flexible styling, you can use CSS-in-JS libraries like Styled-components, Emotion, or JSS. These libraries allow you to write styles directly within your JavaScript code as tagged template literals or functions.

Here's an example using Styled-components:

jsx
```
import styled from 'styled-components';
```

```
const StyledDiv = styled.div`
  background-color: lightblue;
  padding: 10px;
  border: 1px solid #ccc;
`;

class StyledComponent extends React.Component {
  render() {
    return <StyledDiv>Styled Component</StyledDiv>;
  }
}
```

In this code, we define a styled component using Styled-components and apply it to the `div` element. The styles are written using template literals within the tagged `styled.div` template.

CSS Modules

CSS Modules provide a way to encapsulate styles within individual components. With CSS Modules, you can import and use CSS styles as if they were JavaScript objects, ensuring that styles do not leak or conflict with other components.

Here's an example of using CSS Modules in a React component:

jsx
```
import styles from './StyledComponent.module.css';

class StyledComponent extends React.Component {
  render() {
    return <div
className={styles.styledComponent}>Styled
Component</div>;
  }
}
```

In this code, we import a CSS module named `StyledComponent.module.css` and apply the styles using the imported `styles` object.

Summary

Styling in React can be approached in various ways, depending on your project requirements and preferences. Whether you choose to use inline styles, CSS stylesheets, CSS-in-JS libraries, or CSS Modules, React provides the flexibility to implement styling in a way that suits your needs.

By mastering styling techniques in React, you can create visually appealing and well-organized user interfaces that enhance the user experience of your web applications.

React Router: Navigating Your Application

Introduction to React Router

React Router is a powerful library for handling routing and navigation in React applications. Routing is essential when you want to create multi-page experiences within a single-page application (SPA) or when you need to manage different views and components based on the URL.

React Router makes it easy to map specific URLs to different components, allowing you to create a structured and organized navigation system for your application. Whether you're building a simple blog or a complex e-commerce site, React Router is a valuable tool for managing the flow and structure of your app.

Key Concepts

Before diving into React Router, it's essential to understand some key concepts:

1. **Routing:** Routing refers to the process of determining which component or view should be displayed based on the current URL. In React Router, you define routes that specify which components to render for specific URLs.

2. **Single-Page Application (SPA):** A SPA is a web application that loads a single HTML page and dynamically updates its content as the user interacts with the app. React applications are typically SPAs, and React Router helps manage the routing within them.

3. **Components:** In React, each view or page of your application is typically represented by a React component. React Router enables you to map URLs to these components.

4. **Navigation:** Navigation involves moving between different views or pages of your application. React Router provides components like `Link` and methods for programmatic navigation.

React Router Components

React Router offers a set of essential components for building routing into your application:

1. **BrowserRouter:** This component provides the routing infrastructure for your application. It should wrap your entire application to enable routing.

2. **Route:** The `Route` component defines a route and specifies which component should be rendered when the URL matches the route's path.

3. **Link:** The `Link` component creates clickable links that allow users to navigate between different views or pages in your application.

4. **Switch:** The `Switch` component is used to render only the first `Route` that matches the current URL. This prevents multiple routes from rendering simultaneously.

Basic Usage

Here's a basic example of setting up React Router in your application:

jsx
```
import React from 'react';
import { BrowserRouter, Route, Link } from
'react-router-dom';
```

```
function Home() {
  return <h1>Home Page</h1>;
}

function About() {
  return <h1>About Page</h1>;
}

function App() {
  return (
    <BrowserRouter>
      <nav>
        <ul>
          <li><Link to="/">Home</Link></li>
          <li><Link to="/about">About</Link></li>
        </ul>
      </nav>

      <Route exact path="/" component={Home} />
      <Route path="/about" component={About} />
    </BrowserRouter>
  );
}

export default App;
```

In this example, we import React Router components, define two simple components (`Home` and `About`), and set up routing using the `BrowserRouter`, `Route`, and `Link` components.

React Router allows you to create a smooth and interactive user experience by mapping URLs to different views and components in your React application. Whether you're building a small project or a large-scale web app, React Router is a valuable tool for managing navigation and routing.

Summary

React Router is a crucial library for handling routing and navigation in React applications. It simplifies the process of mapping URLs to components, enabling you to create multi-page experiences within a single-page application. Understanding the fundamentals of React Router is essential for building well-structured and navigable web applications.

Basic Routing

Routing is a fundamental concept in web development, allowing you to navigate between different views or pages within your application based on the URL. React Router simplifies the implementation of routing in your React applications by providing a set of components that allow you to define routes and map them to specific components.

Setting Up Basic Routing

To set up basic routing in a React application using React Router, you need to follow these steps:

1. **Installation:** Start by installing React Router using npm or yarn:

bash
```
npm install react-router-dom
# or
yarn add react-router-dom
```

2. **Import Components:** Import the necessary React Router components, such as `BrowserRouter`, `Route`, and `Link`, into your application.

jsx
```
import { BrowserRouter, Route, Link } from 'react-router-dom';
```

3. **Wrap Your App:** Wrap your entire application with the `BrowserRouter` component to enable routing.

jsx

```
<BrowserRouter>
  {/* Your App Components */}
</BrowserRouter>
```

4. **Define Routes:** Use the `Route` component to define routes and specify which component should be rendered when a particular route is matched.

jsx

```
<Route path="/home" component={Home} />
<Route path="/about" component={About} />
```

5. **Create Navigation Links:** Use the `Link` component to create clickable links that allow users to navigate to different routes in your application.

jsx

```
<Link to="/home">Home</Link>
<Link to="/about">About</Link>
```

Example: Basic Routing

Here's a simplified example of basic routing in a React application using React Router:

jsx

```
import React from 'react';
import { BrowserRouter, Route, Link } from
'react-router-dom';

function Home() {
  return <h1>Home Page</h1>;
}
```

```
function About() {
  return <h1>About Page</h1>;
}

function App() {
  return (
    <BrowserRouter>
      <nav>
        <ul>
          <li><Link to="/home">Home</Link></li>
          <li><Link to="/about">About</Link></li>
        </ul>
      </nav>

      <Route path="/home" component={Home} />
      <Route path="/about" component={About} />
    </BrowserRouter>
  );
}

export default App;
```

In this example, we've created a basic React application with two routes: `/home` and `/about`. The `Link` components create navigation links, and the `Route` components define which components should be rendered when these routes are accessed.

When a user clicks the "Home" or "About" link, the corresponding component is displayed in the application, and the URL changes accordingly.

Route Matching

It's important to note that React Router uses a partial match for route paths by default. This means that if you define a route with `path="/home"` and the current URL is `/home/details`, the `Home` component will still be rendered. If you want to enforce exact matches, you can use the `exact` prop like this: `<Route exact path="/home" component={Home} />`.

Summary

Basic routing in React Router allows you to create multi-page experiences within your single-page React application. By defining routes and mapping them to specific components, you can provide users with a structured and navigable user interface. In addition to basic routing, React Router offers advanced features like nested routes, route parameters, and route guards, which enable you to build complex and interactive web applications.

Nested Routes

Nested routes are a powerful feature in React Router that allow you to create complex routing structures within your application. With nested routes, you can render child components within the layout of a parent component, creating a hierarchy of views and enabling more granular control over your application's navigation.

Why Use Nested Routes?

Nested routes are beneficial when you want to:

1. **Organize Layouts:** Create layout components that provide a consistent header, footer, or sidebar for a group of related child components.

2. **Modularize Views:** Divide large views or pages into smaller, reusable components, making your codebase more maintainable.

3. **Granular Navigation:** Enable navigation within a specific section of your application while maintaining the overall structure of your routes.

Setting Up Nested Routes

To set up nested routes in React Router, follow these steps:

1. **Define Parent and Child Components:** Create the parent component that will serve as the layout for the nested routes. Inside this parent component, include a `<Route>` component where the child components will be rendered.

2. **Nest <Route> Components:** Within the parent component, nest additional `<Route>` components to define the child routes. These nested routes should have paths relative to the parent's path.

3. Render Child Routes: In the parent component's render method, use the `children` prop to render the matched child routes.

Example: Nested Routes

Here's an example of setting up nested routes:

jsx
```
import React from 'react';
import { BrowserRouter, Route, Link } from
'react-router-dom';

function Home() {
  return <h1>Home Page</h1>;
}

function Products() {
  return (
    <div>
      <h1>Products Page</h1>
      <ul>
        <li><Link to="/products/product1">Product
1</Link></li>
        <li><Link to="/products/product2">Product
2</Link></li>
      </ul>
    </div>
  );
}

function ProductDetail({ match }) {
  const { productId } = match.params;
  return <h2>Product Detail: {productId}</h2>;
}

function App() {
  return (
```

```
<BrowserRouter>
  <nav>
    <ul>
      <li><Link to="/">Home</Link></li>
      <li><Link
to="/products">Products</Link></li>
    </ul>
  </nav>

  <Route exact path="/" component={Home} />
  <Route path="/products" component={Products}
/>

  {/* Nested Routes */}
  <Route path="/products/:productId"
component={ProductDetail} />
</BrowserRouter>
  );
}

export default App;
```

In this example, the `Products` component serves as the parent for nested routes. Inside the `Products` component, we have links to different product pages (e.g., `/products/product1` and `/products/product2`). The `ProductDetail` component is used to display product details and is nested within the `/products` route.

When you click on a product link, the corresponding `ProductDetail` component is rendered within the layout defined by the `Products` component. This allows you to maintain a consistent layout while displaying dynamic content.

Benefits of Nested Routes

Nested routes enhance code organization, modularity, and maintainability. They provide a clear structure for your application and make it easier to manage complex user interfaces. By nesting routes, you can create a hierarchy of views and components that match the structure of your application.

Summary

Nested routes in React Router enable you to create complex and organized routing structures within your React application. They allow you to divide views into smaller, reusable components, create layout hierarchies, and maintain granular control over navigation. By understanding and using nested routes effectively, you can build more sophisticated and user-friendly web applications.

Route Parameters

Route parameters are a powerful feature in React Router that allow you to capture dynamic segments of a URL and pass them as props to the rendered component. They are useful when you have routes that can vary based on user input, data, or identifiers, such as user profiles, product details, or post IDs.

Using Route Parameters

To use route parameters in React Router, follow these steps:

1. **Define Route with Parameter:** In your route configuration, specify a parameter by placing a colon (`:`) before the parameter name in the route path. For example: `/users/:userId`.

2. **Access Route Parameter:** In the component that corresponds to the route, you can access the route parameter by using the `match.params` object.

Example: Using Route Parameters

Here's an example of how to use route parameters in React Router:

jsx
```
import React from 'react';
import { BrowserRouter, Route, Link } from
'react-router-dom';

function UserProfile({ match }) {
  const { userId } = match.params;
  return <h1>User Profile Page for User ID:
{userId}</h1>;
}
```

```
function App() {
  return (
    <BrowserRouter>
      <nav>
        <ul>
          <li><Link to="/users/123">User
123</Link></li>
          <li><Link to="/users/456">User
456</Link></li>
        </ul>
      </nav>

      <Route path="/users/:userId"
component={UserProfile} />
    </BrowserRouter>
  );
}

export default App;
```

In this example, we've defined a route with a parameter:
`/users/:userId`. When a user clicks a link to a specific user's profile
(e.g., `/users/123` or `/users/456`), the `UserProfile` component is
rendered, and the `userId` parameter is accessible as
`match.params.userId`.

Dynamic Content with Route Parameters

Route parameters enable dynamic content rendering based on the
parameter values. In the example above, the `UserProfile` component
can display user-specific information based on the `userId` parameter.

Route parameters are particularly useful when dealing with data-driven
applications, as they allow you to retrieve data associated with the
parameter value and render it dynamically.

Optional Route Parameters

In addition to required route parameters, you can also define optional route parameters by adding a question mark (`` `?` ``) after the parameter name in the route path. For example: `` `/search/:query?` ``.

Optional parameters allow you to handle routes that may or may not include the parameter value.

Summary

Route parameters in React Router provide a flexible way to capture dynamic segments of URLs and pass them as props to components. They are essential for creating dynamic and data-driven views in your application. Whether you're building user profiles, product details, or search functionality, route parameters are a valuable tool for handling dynamic content and user interactions.

Programmatic Navigation

Programmatic navigation refers to the ability to change the route or URL in your React application using JavaScript code or user interactions, rather than relying solely on clicking links or using the browser's back and forward buttons. React Router provides a `history` object that allows you to programmatically navigate to different routes and control the flow of your application.

Use Cases for Programmatic Navigation

Programmatic navigation is useful in various scenarios:

1. **User Interactions:** You can navigate users to different parts of your application in response to their actions, such as form submissions or button clicks.

2. **Redirects:** You can conditionally redirect users to specific routes based on authentication status, permissions, or other conditions.

3. **Dynamic Routing:** You can navigate to routes with dynamic parameters, such as product details, based on data retrieved from an API.

Using the history Object

The `history` object is a core part of React Router and provides methods to manipulate the browser's history stack and change the route. It can be accessed in different ways:

- **Using Hooks:** You can use the `useHistory` hook to access the `history` object in functional components.

jsx

```jsx
import { useHistory } from 'react-router-dom';

function MyComponent() {
  const history = useHistory();

  function redirectToAboutPage() {
    history.push('/about');
  }

  return (
    <button onClick={redirectToAboutPage}>Go to
About</button>
  );
}
```

- **Using Class Components:** In class components, you can access the `history` object via the `this.props.history` property or by wrapping your component with the `withRouter` higher-order component.

jsx

```jsx
import React from 'react';
import { withRouter } from 'react-router-dom';

class MyComponent extends React.Component {
  redirectToAboutPage = () => {
    this.props.history.push('/about');
  }

  render() {
    return (
      <button
onClick={this.redirectToAboutPage}>Go to
About</button>
    );
  }
}
```

```
export default withRouter(MyComponent);
```

Navigation Methods

The `history` object provides several methods for programmatic navigation:

- **push(path, [state]):** Pushes a new entry onto the history stack, navigating to the specified `path`. You can also include an optional `state` object.

- **replace(path, [state]):** Replaces the current entry on the history stack with the specified `path`. This is similar to `push`, but it replaces the current entry instead of adding a new one.

- **go(n):** Navigates forward or backward in the history stack by `n` steps. A positive `n` moves forward, while a negative `n` moves backward.

- **goBack():** Navigates one step backward in the history stack, equivalent to `go(-1)`.

- `**goForward():** Navigates one step forward in the history stack, equivalent to `go(1)`.

Example: Programmatic Navigation

Here's an example of using programmatic navigation to redirect a user to the "About" page when a button is clicked:

jsx
```jsx
import React from 'react';
import { useHistory } from 'react-router-dom';

function Home() {
  const history = useHistory();
```

```
function redirectToAboutPage() {
  history.push('/about');
}

return (
  <div>
    <h1>Home Page</h1>
    <button onClick={redirectToAboutPage}>Go to
About</button>
  </div>
);
}

export default Home;
```

In this example, the `redirectToAboutPage` function uses the `history.push` method to navigate to the "/about" route when the button is clicked.

Summary

Programmatic navigation is a crucial feature of React Router that allows you to control the flow of your application by changing routes and URLs using JavaScript code. Whether you need to respond to user interactions, conditionally redirect users, or dynamically navigate to routes, programmatic navigation with the `history` object provides the flexibility and control you need to create a smooth and interactive user experience.

Route Guards

Route guards, also known as route protection or navigation guards, are a mechanism in React Router that allows you to control access to specific routes based on conditions or user authentication status. They are essential for securing parts of your application and ensuring that users can only access routes for which they are authorized.

Use Cases for Route Guards

Route guards can be used in various scenarios:

1. **Authentication:** You can use route guards to protect routes that require users to be authenticated. If a user is not logged in, they can be redirected to a login page.

2. **Authorization:** Route guards can enforce authorization rules, ensuring that users have the necessary permissions to access certain routes or resources.

3. **Redirects:** You can use guards for conditional redirects, sending users to different routes based on their context or behavior.

4. **Data Fetching:** Guards can be used to fetch data or perform other actions before a route is rendered, ensuring that data is available when needed.

Implementing Route Guards

In React Router, you can implement route guards by using the following techniques:

1. **Redirects:** You can use the `Redirect` component to programmatically redirect users to a different route. This is often used in conjunction with conditional checks.

jsx
```
import { Redirect } from 'react-router-dom';

function ProtectedRoute({ isAuthenticated,
component: Component, ...rest }) {
    return (
      isAuthenticated ? (
        <Route {...rest} component={Component} />
      ) : (
        <Redirect to="/login" />
      )
    );
}
```

In this example, the `ProtectedRoute` component checks whether the user is authenticated. If they are, it renders the specified `Component`, and if they are not, it redirects to the login page.

2. **Render Props:** You can use the `render` prop of the `Route` component to conditionally render content based on route access.

jsx
```
import { Route } from 'react-router-dom';

function ProtectedRoute({ isAuthenticated,
component: Component, ...rest }) {
    return (
      <Route
        {...rest}
        render={(props) =>
          isAuthenticated ? (
            <Component {...props} />
          ) : (
            <Redirect to="/login" />
          )
        }
      />
```

```
    );
  }
```

This approach is similar to the previous example but uses the `render` prop to conditionally render content.

Example: Implementing Route Guards

Here's an example of implementing a route guard to protect a "Dashboard" route that requires authentication:

jsx
```
import React, { useState } from 'react';
import { BrowserRouter, Route, Redirect, Link } from
'react-router-dom';

function Dashboard() {
  return <h1>Dashboard Page</h1>;
}

function Login({ setIsAuthenticated }) {
  const handleLogin = () => {
    setIsAuthenticated(true);
  };

  return (
    <div>
      <h1>Login Page</h1>
      <button onClick={handleLogin}>Login</button>
    </div>
  );
}

function App() {
  const [isAuthenticated, setIsAuthenticated] =
useState(false);
```

```
return (
  <BrowserRouter>
    <nav>
      <ul>
        <li><Link
to="/dashboard">Dashboard</Link></li>
      </ul>
    </nav>

    <Route path="/dashboard">
      {isAuthenticated ? <Dashboard /> : <Redirect
to="/login" />}
    </Route>
    <Route path="/login">
      <Login
setIsAuthenticated={setIsAuthenticated} />
    </Route>
  </BrowserRouter>
);
}

export default App;
```

In this example, the "Dashboard" route is protected by the `isAuthenticated` state. If the user is authenticated, the `Dashboard` component is rendered; otherwise, they are redirected to the "Login" page.

Summary

Route guards in React Router are crucial for securing parts of your application, enforcing authorization rules, and providing a controlled navigation experience. By implementing guards, you can ensure that users can only access routes they are authorized to use and create a more secure and user-friendly web application. Route guards are essential for building modern and safe web applications, especially those that handle user authentication and authorization.

State Management with Redux

The Need for State Management

In any non-trivial application, managing and sharing state data is a fundamental challenge. State represents the data that your application needs to keep track of, such as user information, application settings, data fetched from APIs, and user interactions. As your application grows in complexity, so does the complexity of handling state.

Here are some key reasons why you need effective state management in your application:

1. **Component Tree Propagation:** In React and other component-based libraries, state is typically localized within individual components. When a piece of state needs to be shared between components that are not directly connected in the component tree, you may encounter problems propagating state up and down the tree.

2. **Global Data:** Some data, like user authentication status or app configuration, needs to be available globally across various parts of your application. Placing this data in an individual component state can lead to redundancy and synchronization issues.

3. **Data Consistency:** Maintaining consistent and synchronized data across different parts of your application can be challenging. State changes in one component may need to trigger updates in multiple other components.

4. **Application Scaling:** As your application grows in complexity, the need for a scalable and organized approach to state management becomes critical. Without a structured solution, your codebase can become difficult to maintain.

5. Debugging and Testing: Effective state management can make debugging and testing easier. Centralized state makes it simpler to inspect and manipulate data during development and testing.

Challenges in State Management

Without a proper state management solution, you might face the following challenges:

1. Prop Drilling: Passing state down through multiple levels of components (prop drilling) can lead to code that's hard to read and maintain.

2. Inconsistent Data: When multiple components have their own copies of the same data, changes in one place may not be reflected elsewhere, leading to inconsistencies.

3. Component Coupling: Sharing state directly between unrelated components can create tight coupling between them, making your code less modular and harder to refactor.

The Role of Redux

Redux is a state management library that addresses these challenges by providing a centralized store for your application's state. It follows the principles of a predictable state container, immutability, and unidirectional data flow.

Introduction to Redux

Redux is an open-source JavaScript library for managing and centralizing the state of your application. It was inspired by the Flux architecture and is often used in conjunction with React, though it can be used with other JavaScript frameworks or libraries as well.

Redux provides a predictable and organized way to handle application state, making it easier to manage data flow and state changes in complex applications. It promotes best practices for state management, such as immutability and a unidirectional data flow.

Core Principles of Redux

Redux is based on a few core principles:

1. **Single Source of Truth:** In Redux, all the application's state is stored in a single JavaScript object called the "store." This means that the entire state of your application is centralized and can be accessed from one place.

2. **Read-Only State:** State in Redux is read-only. You cannot directly modify the state; instead, you dispatch actions to describe state changes.

3. **Pure Functions (Reducers):** State changes in Redux are carried out by pure functions called "reducers." Reducers take the current state and an action as input and return a new state as output. They should be predictable and not have side effects.

4. **Unidirectional Data Flow:** Data flows in one direction in Redux: from the components to the store and back to the components. This unidirectional data flow simplifies data tracking and debugging.

Components of Redux

Redux consists of several key components:

1. **Store:** The store is a plain JavaScript object that holds the entire application's state. You interact with the store using actions and reducers.

2. **Actions:** Actions are objects that describe what should happen in your application. They typically have a `type` property and can also carry additional data.

3. **Reducers:** Reducers are pure functions responsible for handling actions and producing a new state. They specify how the state should change in response to actions.

4. **Middleware:** Middleware in Redux provides a way to intercept and handle actions before they reach the reducers. It's commonly used for side effects, such as making API requests.

Example Usage of Redux

Here's a simplified example of how Redux is used in a React application:

javascript
```
// Define actions
const incrementAction = { type: 'INCREMENT' };
const decrementAction = { type: 'DECREMENT' };

// Define a reducer
const counterReducer = (state = 0, action) => {
  switch (action.type) {
    case 'INCREMENT':
      return state + 1;
    case 'DECREMENT':
```

```
      return state - 1;
    default:
      return state;
  }
};

// Create a Redux store
const { createStore } = Redux;
const store = createStore(counterReducer);

// Dispatch actions to update the state
store.dispatch(incrementAction);
store.dispatch(decrementAction);

// Get the current state from the store
const currentState = store.getState();
console.log(currentState); // Output: 0
```

In this example, we define actions (`incrementAction` and `decrementAction`), create a reducer (`counterReducer`) that specifies how the state should change in response to actions, create a Redux store, dispatch actions to update the state, and retrieve the current state from the store.

Summary

Redux is a powerful library for managing application state by providing a centralized store, a predictable way to handle state changes, and a unidirectional data flow. By following Redux's core principles, you can simplify state management in your applications, improve maintainability, and create more predictable and manageable code. It's particularly valuable for complex applications that require organized and scalable state management.

Actions and Reducers

Actions and reducers are the core building blocks of Redux. They work together to describe how your application's state changes over time and enable predictable state management.

Actions

Actions are plain JavaScript objects that describe what should happen in your application. They convey an intention to change the state. At a minimum, an action typically has a `type` property, which is a string that describes the type of action, and it can also include additional data. Actions are created by action creators, which are functions that return action objects.

javascript
```
// Action creator
function increment() {
  return { type: 'INCREMENT' };
}

// Usage
const action = increment();
// action is { type: 'INCREMENT' }
```

Actions are dispatched to the Redux store to initiate state changes. They are the only source of information for the store about what should happen.

Reducers

Reducers are pure functions that specify how the application's state should change in response to actions. They take the current state and an action as arguments and return a new state. Reducers are responsible for determining how the state transitions from one version to the next.

javascript
```javascript
// Reducer
function counterReducer(state = 0, action) {
  switch (action.type) {
    case 'INCREMENT':
      return state + 1;
    case 'DECREMENT':
      return state - 1;
    default:
      return state;
  }
}

// Usage
const initialState = 0;
const action = { type: 'INCREMENT' };
const newState = counterReducer(initialState,
action);
// newState is 1
```

Key points about reducers:

- They are pure functions and should not have side effects or modify the input data (state).
- They must return a new state object (or the same state object if there's no change).
- They should not modify the original state; instead, they create a copy with the desired changes.

Combining Reducers

In real applications, you may have multiple slices of state, each handled by a different reducer. Redux provides a utility function called `combineReducers` to combine these reducers into a single reducer function.

javascript
```javascript
import { combineReducers } from 'redux';

const rootReducer = combineReducers({
  counter: counterReducer,
  user: userReducer,
  // ... other reducers
});
```

The resulting `rootReducer` can be used to manage the state of the entire application.

Immutable State

Redux encourages the use of immutable state, which means that state objects should not be modified directly. Instead, a new state object is created with the desired changes. This immutability is important for predictability and tracking state changes.

Libraries like Immutable.js or functions like the spread operator (`...`) are often used to create new state objects.

javascript
```javascript
// Immutable state using the spread operator
function counterReducer(state = { count: 0 },
action) {
  switch (action.type) {
    case 'INCREMENT':
      return { ...state, count: state.count + 1 };
    case 'DECREMENT':
      return { ...state, count: state.count - 1 };
    default:
      return state;
```

```
    }
}
```

Summary

Actions and reducers are fundamental concepts in Redux that enable a predictable and organized way to manage state in your application. Actions describe changes in the state, while reducers specify how those changes are applied to the state. By following these patterns and principles, Redux provides a structured and maintainable approach to state management, making it easier to reason about and manage state changes as your application grows in complexity.

Connecting Redux to React

Redux provides a centralized store and a predictable way to handle state changes, but to make it work seamlessly with React, you need to establish a connection between the two libraries. This connection involves integrating Redux into your React components so they can access and update the state managed by Redux.

React-Redux Library

To connect Redux with React, you can use the "react-redux" library, which provides a set of utilities to simplify the integration. The two main components from "react-redux" that facilitate this connection are:

1. **<Provider> Component:** The `<Provider>` component is a higher-order component (HOC) that wraps your entire React application. It makes the Redux store available to all components in the application, allowing them to access the store's state.

2. **connect() Function:** The `connect()` function is used to create container components that can read data from the Redux store and dispatch actions. It connects your React components to the Redux store, enabling them to interact with Redux state and actions.

Using <Provider> Component

To use the `<Provider>` component, wrap your root component (usually `App`) with it. This provides the Redux store to all components in your application.

javascript
```
import React from 'react';
import ReactDOM from 'react-dom';
import { Provider } from 'react-redux';
import App from './App';
```

```
import store from './store';

ReactDOM.render(
  <Provider store={store}>
    <App />
  </Provider>,
  document.getElementById('root')
);
```

In this example, `store` is the Redux store you created using the `createStore()` function.

Using connect() Function

To connect individual components to Redux, use the `connect()` function. It is typically applied to a component and takes two functions as arguments:

- mapStateToProps: This function maps the Redux store's state to props that the connected component can access.

- mapDispatchToProps: This function maps Redux action creators to props that the connected component can use to dispatch actions.

Here's an example of connecting a component to Redux:

javascript
```
import React from 'react';
import { connect } from 'react-redux';

class Counter extends React.Component {
  render() {
    return (
      <div>
        <p>Count: {this.props.count}</p>
```

```
          <button
onClick={this.props.increment}>Increment</button>
          <button
onClick={this.props.decrement}>Decrement</button>
        </div>
      );
    }
}


const mapStateToProps = (state) => {
  return {
    count: state.counter, // "counter" is a key in
the Redux store
    };
};


const mapDispatchToProps = (dispatch) => {
  return {
    increment: () => dispatch({ type: 'INCREMENT'
}),
    decrement: () => dispatch({ type: 'DECREMENT'
}),
    };
};


export default connect(mapStateToProps,
mapDispatchToProps)(Counter);
```

In this example, `connect()` connects the `Counter` component to
Redux by mapping the `count` state and the `increment` and
`decrement` actions to its props.

Accessing Redux State in Connected Components

Once connected, you can access Redux state in your connected
components using the props defined in the `mapStateToProps` function.

In the example above, `this.props.count` gives you access to the `counter` state from the Redux store.

Dispatching Actions in Connected Components

Similarly, you can dispatch Redux actions in your connected components using the props defined in the `mapDispatchToProps` function. In the example above, `this.props.increment()` and `this.props.decrement()` are functions that dispatch the corresponding actions.

Summary

Connecting Redux to React using the "react-redux" library allows you to seamlessly integrate Redux state management into your React application. The `<Provider>` component makes the Redux store available to all components, while the `connect()` function creates container components that can access the store's state and dispatch actions. This integration simplifies the way React components interact with Redux, making it easier to manage and update application state.

Redux Middleware

Redux Middleware is a powerful feature that allows you to intercept and handle actions before they reach the reducers or after they leave the reducers. Middleware provides a way to add additional functionality to Redux, such as logging, asynchronous operations, and more, while keeping your reducers pure and focused on state management.

Middleware functions are executed in the order they are applied, allowing you to create a pipeline of actions that flow through each middleware before reaching the reducers.

Common Use Cases for Middleware

Middleware can be used for a variety of purposes:

1. **Logging:** Middleware can log actions, state changes, or errors for debugging and monitoring purposes.

2. **Asynchronous Operations:** Middleware can handle asynchronous actions, such as making API requests, and dispatching new actions when the asynchronous operation completes.

3. **Authentication and Authorization:** Middleware can check user authentication or authorization before allowing certain actions to proceed.

4. **Caching:** Middleware can cache data to improve performance or reduce unnecessary network requests.

Creating Custom Middleware

You can create custom middleware functions to extend Redux's functionality to meet your application's specific needs. A middleware function receives three arguments:

- **store:** The Redux store instance, which provides access to state and the `dispatch` function.

- **next:** A function that passes the action to the next middleware in the chain. If there are no more middleware functions, it passes the action to the reducers.

- **action:** The action object that was dispatched.

Here's a basic example of a custom middleware that logs actions:

javascript
```
const loggerMiddleware = (store) => (next) =>
(action) => {
  console.log('Action:', action);
  return next(action);
};
```

You can apply this middleware to your Redux store using the `applyMiddleware` function from the Redux library:

javascript
```
import { createStore, applyMiddleware } from
'redux';
import rootReducer from './reducers';

const store = createStore(
  rootReducer,
  applyMiddleware(loggerMiddleware)
);
```

In this example, the `loggerMiddleware` logs actions before passing them to the next middleware or reducers.

Async Actions with Redux Thunk

For handling asynchronous operations, Redux provides an excellent middleware library called Redux Thunk. Redux Thunk allows you to dispatch functions as actions in addition to plain objects. These functions can perform asynchronous tasks and dispatch new actions when they're done.

Here's an example of how to use Redux Thunk for making an asynchronous API request:

javascript
```javascript
import { createStore, applyMiddleware } from
'redux';
import thunk from 'redux-thunk';
import rootReducer from './reducers';

const store = createStore(
  rootReducer,
  applyMiddleware(thunk)
);

const fetchUserData = (userId) => {
  return (dispatch) => {
    dispatch({ type: 'FETCH_USER_REQUEST' });

    // Perform an asynchronous operation, e.g.,
fetch data from an API
    fetch(`/api/users/${userId}`)
      .then((response) => response.json())
      .then((data) => {
        dispatch({ type: 'FETCH_USER_SUCCESS',
payload: data });
      })
      .catch((error) => {
        dispatch({ type: 'FETCH_USER_FAILURE',
payload: error });
      });
  };
```

```
};

// Dispatch the async action
store.dispatch(fetchUserData(123));
```

In this example, the `fetchUserData` function is a Redux Thunk action that dispatches three actions: one for the request, one for success, and one for failure.

Summary

Redux Middleware is a powerful feature that extends Redux's capabilities by allowing you to intercept, process, and modify actions as they flow through your application. Custom middleware functions can be created to handle specific tasks like logging, authentication, or caching. Additionally, Redux Thunk provides a way to manage asynchronous operations in Redux by allowing you to dispatch functions as actions. Middleware plays a crucial role in enhancing the functionality and flexibility of Redux for various use cases in your applications.

Organizing Redux Code

Organizing your Redux code effectively is crucial for maintainability and scalability as your application grows. Redux doesn't prescribe a specific folder structure or organization, but there are common patterns and best practices that you can follow to keep your Redux code organized and structured.

Folder Structure

A well-defined folder structure can help you keep your Redux code organized and easy to navigate. While there are different approaches, here's a common folder structure for a Redux-based application:

```
src/
  actions/
  reducers/
  store/
  middleware/
```

- **actions/**: This folder contains action creators and action type constants. Each action creator function typically corresponds to a specific action that can be dispatched.

- **reducers/**: The `reducers/` folder contains reducer functions that handle state changes for different parts of your application. It's common to have one reducer file per feature or slice of state.

- **store/**: Here, you configure and create your Redux store. This folder may also include store-related files, such as the root reducer.

- **middleware/:** Middleware functions, if used, can be organized in this folder.

Separation by Feature

An alternative approach to organizing Redux code is to structure your folders by feature, especially if your application is divided into distinct features or modules. In this structure, each feature has its own folder containing action creators, reducers, and selectors.

```
src/
  feature1/
    actions/
    reducers/
    selectors/
  feature2/
    actions/
    reducers/
    selectors/
  ...
```

This approach can make it easier to manage code related to a specific feature and minimize the impact of changes in one feature on the rest of the application.

Use Ducks Pattern (Optional)

The "Ducks" pattern is an alternative way to organize Redux code that encapsulates related actions and reducers into a single module. This pattern can simplify the code structure, especially in smaller applications.

Here's a simplified example of the Ducks pattern:

javascript
```
// featureDuck.js

// Action Types
```

```
const INCREMENT = 'feature/INCREMENT';
const DECREMENT = 'feature/DECREMENT';

// Reducer
export default function reducer(state = 0, action) {
  switch (action.type) {
    case INCREMENT:
      return state + 1;
    case DECREMENT:
      return state - 1;
    default:
      return state;
  }
}

// Action Creators
export function increment() {
  return { type: INCREMENT };
}

export function decrement() {
  return { type: DECREMENT };
}
```

This pattern places related actions, action types, and the reducer together in a single module.

Selectors

Selectors are functions that allow you to access specific pieces of state from the Redux store. It's a good practice to define selectors for each part of the state you need to access in your components. Selectors can be organized in their own folder or grouped with the related feature.

Summary

Organizing Redux code effectively is essential for maintaining a clean and manageable codebase as your application grows. The choice of folder structure and organization approach depends on the specific needs of your application. Whether you use a folder structure based on features or modules, the Ducks pattern, or another approach, the goal is to keep your Redux code organized, modular, and easy to maintain. Consistency and clear separation of concerns are key principles to follow when organizing Redux code in your application.

Hooks: Simplifying Component Logic

Introduction to Hooks

Hooks are a powerful addition to React that simplify the management of component logic and state. They were introduced in React 16.8 as a way to use state and other React features without writing class components. Hooks allow you to reuse stateful logic across components and streamline the development process.

Before hooks, managing state and lifecycle events in React typically required class components. With hooks, functional components can handle these responsibilities, making them more versatile and expressive.

Why Hooks?

Hooks were introduced to address several issues with class components:

1. **Complexity:** Class components could become complex and harder to understand as logic related to state, lifecycle methods, and side effects piled up.

2. **Reusability:** Sharing logic between components often required higher-order components (HOCs) or render props, which could lead to nesting and less readable code.

3. **Learning Curve:** Class components, especially for beginners, could be challenging to learn due to the intricacies of the `this` keyword and lifecycle methods.

Core Hooks

React comes with several built-in hooks that cover a range of use cases:

1. **useState():** This hook allows functional components to manage local component state. It returns an array with the current state value and a function to update it.

2. **useEffect():** This hook replaces lifecycle methods (such as `componentDidMount`, `componentDidUpdate`, and `componentWillUnmount`) and is used for handling side effects in functional components.

3. **useContext():** This hook allows you to access the context of a parent component. It's often used in conjunction with the Context API for managing global state.

4. **useReducer():** This hook is used for managing more complex state logic when `useState` isn't sufficient. It follows the same pattern as the Redux reducer.

5. **useRef():** This hook provides access to a mutable ref object that can be used to access the DOM or store values that persist between renders without causing re-renders.

6. **useMemo() and useCallback():** These hooks are used for memoization and performance optimization. They help prevent unnecessary calculations and function re-creations.

7. **Custom Hooks:** You can create your own custom hooks to encapsulate reusable logic and share it across components. Custom hooks often begin with the `use` prefix, like `useCustomHook()`.

Using Hooks

To use hooks, you import them from the React library and call them within your functional components. Here's an example using the `useState` hook:

javascript
```javascript
import React, { useState } from 'react';

function Counter() {
  const [count, setCount] = useState(0);

  return (
    <div>
      <p>Count: {count}</p>
      <button onClick={() => setCount(count +
1)}>Increment</button>
    </div>
  );
}
```

In this example, the `useState` hook initializes the `count` state variable to `0` and provides the `setCount` function to update it.

Hooks have revolutionized how developers write React components, making them more concise, readable, and maintainable. They enable functional components to manage state and side effects effectively, eliminating the need for class components in many cases.

Summary

Hooks are a valuable addition to React that simplify component logic by allowing functional components to manage state, side effects, and other features that were traditionally associated with class components. With a set of core hooks and the ability to create custom hooks, you can build cleaner, more modular, and reusable components in your React applications.

`useState` Hook

The `useState` Hook is one of the most fundamental and widely used hooks in React. It allows functional components to manage local state, which was previously the domain of class components. With `useState`, you can easily add and manipulate state variables within your functional components.

Using `useState`

To use the `useState` Hook, you need to import it from the React library. Here's the basic syntax:

javascript
```javascript
import React, { useState } from 'react';

function ExampleComponent() {
  // Declare a state variable, initialize it with a
default value
  const [stateVariable, setStateVariable] =
useState(initialValue);

  // ...
}
```

- **stateVariable**: This is the state variable you want to manage within your component. It represents a piece of state data.

- **setStateVariable**: This is a function that you can use to update the value of `stateVariable`. It takes a new value as an argument and triggers a re-render of your component with the updated state.

- **initialValue**: This is the initial value of your state variable. It can be a primitive value (e.g., string, number, boolean) or an initial state object.

Example of `useState`

Here's a simple example of how to use the `useState` Hook to manage a counter in a functional component:

javascript
```
import React, { useState } from 'react';

function Counter() {
  // Initialize the state variable "count" with an
initial value of 0
  const [count, setCount] = useState(0);

  // Event handler to increment the count
  const increment = () => {
    setCount(count + 1);
  };

  return (
    <div>
      <p>Count: {count}</p>
      <button onClick={increment}>Increment</button>
    </div>
  );
}
```

In this example, we start with an initial state of `0` and use the `setCount` function to update the `count` state variable when the "Increment" button is clicked. The new value is calculated based on the current value of `count`, ensuring that state updates are not lost.

Multiple State Variables

You can use `useState` multiple times within a single component to manage multiple state variables independently. Each call to `useState` creates a new state variable and its corresponding update function.

javascript
```
import React, { useState } from 'react';

function Form() {
  const [name, setName] = useState('');
  const [email, setEmail] = useState('');

  // ...
}
```

This allows you to manage different pieces of state in a modular and organized manner.

Previous State in `setState`

The `setState` function returned by `useState` can also take a function as an argument. This function receives the previous state as its argument, making it safer for managing state updates that depend on the current state.

javascript
```
const [count, setCount] = useState(0);

// Using previous state to increment count
const increment = () => {
  setCount((prevCount) => prevCount + 1);
};
```

Using the previous state ensures that you're working with the most up-to-date state value, especially in scenarios with asynchronous updates.

Summary

The `useState` Hook is a fundamental part of React's modern functional component approach. It allows you to manage state within your components, making them more flexible and expressive. By calling `useState`, you can declare state variables and update them with the corresponding state-setting function. This enables you to build dynamic and interactive components with ease.

`useEffect` Hook

The `useEffect` Hook is a vital part of React's hook system, allowing functional components to handle side effects and manage component lifecycle events. It replaces the lifecycle methods (`componentDidMount`, `componentDidUpdate`, and `componentWillUnmount`) in class components.

Purpose of `useEffect`

`useEffect` is used to perform side effects in your functional components. Side effects include data fetching, DOM manipulation, subscriptions, and other operations that can't or shouldn't be done directly in the render function.

Using `useEffect`

To use the `useEffect` Hook, you need to import it from the React library. The basic syntax is as follows:

javascript
```javascript
import React, { useEffect } from 'react';

function ExampleComponent() {
  useEffect(() => {
    // Side effect code goes here
  }, [dependencyArray]);

  // ...
}
```

- The first argument to `useEffect` is a function that contains the code for the side effect you want to perform.

- The second argument is an optional dependency array. It's an array of values (often props or state variables) that, when changed, will trigger the execution of the effect. If the dependency array is empty (`[]`), the effect runs only once when the component mounts.

Example of `useEffect`

Here's a simple example of how to use the `useEffect` Hook to perform a side effect when the component mounts:

javascript
```
import React, { useState, useEffect } from 'react';

function ExampleComponent() {
  const [count, setCount] = useState(0);

  useEffect(() => {
    document.title = `Count: ${count}`;
  }, [count]);

  return (
    <div>
      <p>Count: {count}</p>
      <button onClick={() => setCount(count +
1)}>Increment</button>
    </div>
  );
}
```

In this example, the effect sets the document title to reflect the current count value. The effect is triggered whenever the `count` state variable changes, ensuring that the document title stays in sync with the component's state.

Cleanup in `useEffect`

`useEffect` allows you to return a cleanup function from the effect if needed. This function is executed when the component is unmounted or when the dependencies specified in the dependency array change.

javascript
```javascript
useEffect(() => {
  // Side effect code goes here

  return () => {
    // Cleanup code goes here
  };
}, [dependencyArray]);
```

Cleanup functions are commonly used to unsubscribe from subscriptions, close connections, or perform other necessary cleanup tasks to prevent memory leaks and unexpected behavior.

Multiple `useEffect` Calls

You can use multiple `useEffect` calls within the same component to organize different side effects. Each `useEffect` is independent and manages its own side effect logic.

javascript
```javascript
useEffect(() => {
  // Effect 1
}, [dependency1]);

useEffect(() => {
  // Effect 2
}, [dependency2]);
```

This allows you to keep related logic together and separate concerns in your component.

Summary

The `useEffect` Hook is a crucial tool for managing side effects and lifecycle events in functional components. It replaces lifecycle methods and provides a cleaner and more expressive way to handle asynchronous operations, data fetching, DOM manipulation, and more. By specifying dependencies, you can control when the effect runs, ensuring that your component's behavior remains predictable and efficient.

`useContext` Hook

The `useContext` Hook is a valuable addition to React that simplifies the process of consuming context in functional components. It provides a straightforward way to access values from the context object without the need for a higher-order component (HOC) or render props.

Context in React

Context in React is a way to share data between components without the need to pass props manually through every level of the component tree. Context is often used for providing global state, themes, authentication, and other data that many components need access to.

Using useContext

To use the `useContext` Hook, you need to import it from the React library. The basic syntax is as follows:

javascript
```javascript
import React, { useContext } from 'react';

function ExampleComponent() {
  const contextValue = useContext(ContextObject);

  // ...
}
```

- **ContextObject**: This is the context object created using `React.createContext()`. It represents the context you want to access.

Example of `useContext`

Here's a simple example of how to use the `useContext` Hook to access a theme context:

javascript
```javascript
import React, { useContext } from 'react';

// Create a context object
const ThemeContext = React.createContext('light');

function ThemedText() {
  // Use the useContext Hook to access the current
theme value
  const theme = useContext(ThemeContext);

  return <p className={`theme-${theme}`}>Themed
Text</p>;
}

function ExampleComponent() {
  return (
    <div>
      <ThemedText />
    </div>
  );
}
```

In this example, the `ThemedText` component uses the `useContext` Hook to access the current theme value from the `ThemeContext`. This allows the component to render the text with the appropriate theme class.

Nested Contexts

You can also use multiple context objects in nested components. Each context object provides its own set of values, and the `useContext` Hook allows you to access the values from the nearest context up the component tree.

javascript
```javascript
import React, { useContext } from 'react';

const ThemeContext = React.createContext('light');
const UserContext = React.createContext('Guest');

function Profile() {
  const theme = useContext(ThemeContext);
  const user = useContext(UserContext);

  return (
    <div className={`theme-${theme}`}>
      <p>Welcome, {user}!</p>
    </div>
  );
}

function App() {
  return (
    <ThemeContext.Provider value="dark">
      <UserContext.Provider value="John">
        <Profile />
      </UserContext.Provider>
    </ThemeContext.Provider>
  );
}
```

In this example, the `Profile` component uses both the `ThemeContext` and `UserContext` to render the user's profile with the appropriate theme and username.

Summary

The `useContext` Hook is a valuable tool for consuming context values in functional components. It simplifies the process of accessing context data, making your code cleaner and more readable. By using the `useContext` Hook, you can efficiently access global state, themes, authentication, and other context values, reducing the need for prop drilling and making your components more flexible and modular.

Custom Hooks

Custom Hooks are a powerful feature introduced in React that enables you to encapsulate and reuse component logic across different parts of your application. They are regular JavaScript functions that start with the word "use" and can use built-in hooks as building blocks. Custom Hooks allow you to abstract complex logic, promote reusability, and make your codebase cleaner and more maintainable.

Creating Custom Hooks

To create a custom hook, follow these steps:

1. **Define a Function**: Start by defining a JavaScript function. The function can accept parameters to customize its behavior.

2. **Use Built-in Hooks**: Inside your custom hook, you can use built-in hooks like `useState`, `useEffect`, or other custom hooks you've created.

3. **Return Values**: Custom hooks should return the data or functionality that other components need.

Here's an example of a custom hook called `useCounter` that encapsulates counter functionality:

javascript
```javascript
import { useState } from 'react';

function useCounter(initialValue = 0, step = 1) {
  const [count, setCount] = useState(initialValue);

  const increment = () => {
    setCount(count + step);
  };

  const decrement = () => {
    setCount(count - step);
```

```
  };

  return {
    count,
    increment,
    decrement,
  };
}

export default useCounter;
```

In this example, `useCounter` is a custom hook that manages a counter state and provides functions to increment and decrement it. It returns an object with the `count`, `increment`, and `decrement` values.

Using Custom Hooks

Using custom hooks in your components is straightforward. You import the custom hook and call it within a functional component:

javascript
```
import React from 'react';
import useCounter from './useCounter';

function Counter() {
  const { count, increment, decrement } =
useCounter();

  return (
    <div>
      <p>Count: {count}</p>
      <button onClick={increment}>Increment</button>
      <button onClick={decrement}>Decrement</button>
    </div>
  );
}
```

In this example, the `Counter` component uses the `useCounter` custom hook to manage the counter state and provide increment and decrement functionality.

Benefits of Custom Hooks

Custom Hooks offer several advantages:

1. **Reusability:** You can reuse custom hooks in multiple components, promoting code reuse and maintainability.

2. **Abstraction:** Custom hooks allow you to abstract complex logic, making your components cleaner and more focused on presentation.

3. **Testing:** Custom hooks can be tested independently, simplifying unit testing for your application logic.

4. **Separation of Concerns:** Custom hooks help separate concerns, keeping your components focused on rendering and presentation while handling logic separately.

Common Use Cases

Custom hooks can be used for various purposes, including:

- **State Management:** Managing and sharing state logic across components.

- **Data Fetching:** Abstracting data fetching and API calls.

- **Form Handling:** Simplifying form validation and submission logic.

- **Authentication:** Handling user authentication and authorization.

- **Local Storage:** Abstracting local storage interactions.

- **Animation:** Managing animations and transitions.

- **Navigation:** Handling routing and navigation.

By creating custom hooks tailored to your application's needs, you can significantly improve code organization, reusability, and maintainability.

Summary

Custom Hooks are a powerful feature in React that allows you to encapsulate and reuse component logic effectively. By creating custom hooks, you can abstract complex logic into reusable functions, promote code reuse, and keep your components focused on presentation. Custom Hooks are a valuable addition to your React development toolkit and can simplify various aspects of your application development.

Common Custom Hooks

Custom Hooks are a powerful way to abstract and reuse component logic in your React applications. They allow you to encapsulate stateful logic, side effects, and more into reusable functions that can be shared across components.

Creating Custom Hooks

To create a custom hook, follow these steps:

1. **Start with "use"**: Custom Hooks conventionally start with the word "use" to make it clear that they follow the Hook pattern.

2. **Extract Logic**: Identify the logic you want to encapsulate and extract it into a function.

3. **Use Built-in Hooks**: Custom Hooks often use built-in Hooks like `useState`, `useEffect`, or `useContext` to manage state and side effects.

4. **Return Values**: A custom Hook should return any values that other components need to use.

Here's an example of a custom Hook called `useLocalStorage` that simplifies reading and writing data to the local storage:

javascript
```javascript
import { useState } from 'react';

function useLocalStorage(key, initialValue) {
  // Get the stored value from local storage, or use
the initial value
  const [storedValue, setStoredValue] = useState(()
=> {
    const item = window.localStorage.getItem(key);
    return item ? JSON.parse(item) : initialValue;
  });
```

```
  // Update the local storage when the value changes
  const setValue = (value) => {
    setStoredValue(value);
    window.localStorage.setItem(key,
JSON.stringify(value));
  };

  return [storedValue, setValue];
}

export default useLocalStorage;
```

This custom Hook encapsulates the logic for reading and writing data to local storage. It uses `useState` to manage the state and provides a function to update the stored value.

Using Custom Hooks

Once you've created a custom Hook, you can use it in any functional component just like any other Hook. Here's an example of how to use the `useLocalStorage` Hook:

javascript
```
import React from 'react';
import useLocalStorage from './useLocalStorage';

function ExampleComponent() {
  // Use the custom Hook to get and set a value in
local storage
  const [name, setName] =
useLocalStorage('username', 'Guest');

  return (
    <div>
      <p>Welcome, {name}!</p>
```

```
    <input
      type="text"
      value={name}
      onChange={(e) => setName(e.target.value)}
    />
  </div>
  );
}
```

In this example, the `useLocalStorage` Hook simplifies the process of managing local storage for the "username" value. It provides a state variable `name` and a function `setName` for updating the value.

Benefits of Custom Hooks

Custom Hooks offer several benefits:

1. **Reusability**: You can reuse the same custom Hook in multiple components, promoting code reuse and maintainability.

2. **Abstraction**: Custom Hooks allow you to abstract complex logic and make it easier to understand and manage.

3. **Separation of Concerns**: Custom Hooks help separate concerns, keeping your components focused on rendering and presentation while handling logic separately.

4. **Testing**: Custom Hooks can be tested independently, making it easier to write unit tests for your application logic.

Common Custom Hooks

There are numerous scenarios where custom Hooks can be helpful:

- **Data Fetching:** Custom Hooks can encapsulate data fetching logic using APIs like `fetch` or libraries like Axios.

- **Authentication:** Custom Hooks can handle user authentication and authorization logic.

- **Form Handling:** Custom Hooks can simplify form validation and submission.

- **State Management:** Custom Hooks can provide shared state management for various components.

- **Animation:** Custom Hooks can manage animations and transitions.

- **Navigation:** Custom Hooks can simplify routing and navigation.

- **Theming:** Custom Hooks can handle theme management and switching.

- **Local Storage and Session Storage:** Custom Hooks can abstract local and session storage interactions.

By creating custom Hooks tailored to your application's needs, you can significantly improve code organization, reusability, and maintainability.

Summary

Custom Hooks are a powerful way to encapsulate and share component logic in React applications. By following the Hook pattern and creating reusable functions, you can abstract complex logic, improve code organization, and make your components more modular and maintainable. Custom Hooks can simplify various aspects of your application, from data fetching to state management, and can be a valuable addition to your React development toolkit.

Advanced Topics in React

Error Handling and Error Boundaries

Error handling is a crucial aspect of building robust and user-friendly applications in React. Errors can occur in various parts of your application, from unexpected API responses to runtime issues. React provides a mechanism called "Error Boundaries" to gracefully handle errors and prevent them from crashing your entire application.

Error Boundaries

An Error Boundary is a React component that can catch JavaScript errors anywhere within its child component tree, log those errors, and display a fallback UI to the user. Error Boundaries are regular React components that define two special lifecycle methods: `componentDidCatch` and `getDerivedStateFromError`.

1. `**componentDidCatch(error, info)**`: This method is called when an error occurs in any of the child components. It receives two arguments: the error that was thrown and an object containing additional information about the error.

2. `**getDerivedStateFromError(error)**`: This static method is used to update the component's state based on the error that occurred. It should return an object that updates the state.

Using Error Boundaries

You can create Error Boundaries as regular React components and wrap them around the parts of your application where you want to handle errors. Here's an example of how to define an Error Boundary component:

javascript

```javascript
import React, { Component } from 'react';

class ErrorBoundary extends Component {
  constructor(props) {
    super(props);
    this.state = { hasError: false };
  }

  componentDidCatch(error, info) {
    // Log the error to an error reporting service
    console.error('Error:', error);
    console.error('Error Info:', info);
    // Set the state to indicate that an error
occurred
    this.setState({ hasError: true });
  }

  render() {
    if (this.state.hasError) {
      // Display a fallback UI when an error occurs
      return <div>Something went wrong.</div>;
    }
    return this.props.children;
  }
}

export default ErrorBoundary;
```

In this example, the `ErrorBoundary` component defines `componentDidCatch` to log errors and set the `hasError` state to `true` when an error occurs. It also provides a fallback UI to display when an error is caught.

You can use this Error Boundary by wrapping it around components that might throw errors:

javascript
```
<ErrorBoundary>
  <ComponentThatMightThrowErrors />
</ErrorBoundary>
```

Handling Errors Gracefully

When an Error Boundary catches an error, it provides an opportunity to handle the error gracefully. You can log the error, display a user-friendly message, and allow the rest of your application to continue functioning.

Here are some common strategies for handling errors:

- **Logging:** Use `console.error` or send error reports to a logging service to track and diagnose issues.

- **Fallback UI:** Display a user-friendly message or a fallback UI when an error occurs, preventing a broken user experience.

- **Retry Mechanism:** Implement a retry mechanism to retry failed operations, such as fetching data, before showing an error message.

- **User Feedback:** Provide a way for users to report errors or issues they encounter.

Error Handling Best Practices

1. **Use Error Boundaries Wisely:** Don't wrap your entire application in Error Boundaries. Instead, identify specific parts of your UI where errors might occur and wrap those components.

2. **Keep Error Boundaries Simple:** Error Boundaries should focus on error handling and logging, not on complex UI or business logic.

3. **Test Error Handling:** Write tests to ensure that your Error Boundaries behave as expected when errors occur.

4. **Understand Error Propagation:** Errors caught by an Error Boundary do not propagate to other Error Boundaries. You can have multiple Error Boundaries in your app to handle errors in different parts of the UI.

5. **Global Error Handling:** Consider implementing global error handling mechanisms like window.onerror to capture unhandled JavaScript errors.

6. **Regularly Review Logs:** Pay attention to error logs and reports to identify and address issues in your application.

Summary

Error handling and Error Boundaries are essential tools for building robust React applications. Error Boundaries allow you to catch and handle errors gracefully, preventing your application from crashing and providing a better user experience. By strategically placing Error Boundaries and following best practices, you can ensure that your application handles errors effectively and remains reliable.

Portals

Portals are a powerful feature in React that allow you to render a component's children into a different part of the DOM hierarchy than where the component is defined. This can be particularly useful for scenarios where you need to render content outside the normal document flow or into a different DOM element, such as modals, tooltips, or dropdown menus.

Why Use Portals?

Portals provide several advantages:

1. **DOM Structure Control:** Portals allow you to control the placement of your component's content in the DOM, which can be useful for situations where you need to render outside the normal document flow.

2. **Layering:** You can use portals to render content above other elements on the page, such as modal dialogs or tooltips, without worrying about z-index or CSS conflicts.

3. **Separation of Concerns:** Portals allow you to separate the rendering logic of a component from its positioning in the DOM, promoting better code organization.

Creating a Portal

To create a portal in React, you use the `ReactDOM.createPortal()` method. Here's the basic syntax:

javascript
```
import ReactDOM from 'react-dom';

ReactDOM.createPortal(child, container)
```

- `child`: The component or element you want to render in the portal.

- `container`: A reference to a DOM element where you want to render the `child` component.

Example of Using Portals

Here's an example of how to use portals to render a modal dialog outside the normal document flow:

javascript
```javascript
import React from 'react';
import ReactDOM from 'react-dom';

function Modal(props) {
  const modalRoot =
document.getElementById('modal-root');

  return ReactDOM.createPortal(
    <div className="modal">
      <div className="modal-content">
        {props.children}
      </div>
    </div>,
    modalRoot
  );
}

function App() {
  return (
    <div>
      <h1>My App</h1>
      <Modal>
        <p>This is a modal dialog</p>
      </Modal>
    </div>
```

```
  );
}

ReactDOM.render(<App />,
document.getElementById('root'));
```

In this example, the `Modal` component renders its content as a portal into the `modal-root` DOM element, which is separate from the main `root` element of the application. This allows the modal to appear above the main content and outside the normal document flow.

Best Practices for Portals

When using portals, consider the following best practices:

1. **Create a Portal Container:** It's a good practice to create a separate DOM element (e.g., `modal-root`) for portals in your HTML structure. This keeps your portals organized and simplifies cleanup.

2. **Cleanup After Unmount:** Ensure that you clean up your portals when they are unmounted to prevent memory leaks. You can do this by using lifecycle methods or React hooks like `useEffect`.

3. **Accessibility:** Ensure that your portals are accessible to users with disabilities by managing focus, handling keyboard interactions, and providing proper ARIA attributes.

4. **Testing:** Test portals thoroughly, especially their interaction with other components and events.

Summary

Portals in React provide a powerful way to render components outside their normal DOM hierarchy. They are particularly useful for scenarios like modals, tooltips, and dropdown menus, where you need precise control over the rendering location. By using portals, you can enhance the user experience and keep your code organized and maintainable.

Higher-Order Components (HOCs)

Higher-Order Components (HOCs) are a design pattern in React that allows you to reuse component logic, share code between components, and add additional functionality to your React components. HOCs are not a built-in feature of React but rather a pattern that leverages the composability of React components.

Understanding HOCs

The concept of HOCs can be understood as follows:

- A Higher-Order Component is a function that takes a component and returns a new enhanced component.

- HOCs allow you to wrap one or more components with additional logic or behavior.

- HOCs are used to abstract and share common functionality or state management between components.

Creating a Higher-Order Component

To create a Higher-Order Component, you define a function that takes a component as an argument and returns a new component with additional props, state, or behavior. Here's a simplified example:

javascript
```javascript
function withLogging(WrappedComponent) {
  return class extends React.Component {
    componentDidMount() {
      console.log(`Component
${WrappedComponent.name} mounted.`);
    }
```

```
  render() {
    return <WrappedComponent {...this.props} />;
  }
};
}
```

In this example, `withLogging` is a HOC that adds logging functionality to any component passed as an argument. The returned component logs a message when it mounts and then renders the wrapped component.

Using a Higher-Order Component

You can use a HOC by wrapping a component with the HOC function. Here's an example of how to use the `withLogging` HOC:

javascript
```
const EnhancedComponent = withLogging(MyComponent);
```

In this example, `EnhancedComponent` is the result of wrapping `MyComponent` with the `withLogging` HOC. `EnhancedComponent` will have the additional logging behavior.

Common Use Cases for HOCs

HOCs are versatile and can be used for various purposes, including:

1. **Code Reuse:** Share common functionality like authentication, logging, or data fetching between components.

2. **Props Manipulation:** Add or modify props before passing them to a component.

3. **Conditional Rendering:** Conditionally render components based on specific criteria or user permissions.

4. **State Management:** Share state logic, such as managing form state, between multiple components.

5. **Performance Enhancements:** Optimize rendering behavior, such as memoization or data caching.

HOC Composition

You can compose multiple HOCs to create more complex behaviors or combinations of functionality. For example:

javascript
```
const EnhancedComponent =
withLogging(withAuthentication(MyComponent));
```

In this example, `EnhancedComponent` is the result of composing the `withLogging` and `withAuthentication` HOCs.

Caveats and Considerations

While HOCs are a powerful pattern, there are some considerations to keep in mind:

1. **Props Proxying:** Ensure that you properly pass props to the wrapped component, including handling all lifecycle methods and passing through props without affecting their names or values.

2. **Component Identity:** HOCs create new components, which can impact component identity. You may need to use tools like React DevTools to inspect component hierarchies.

3. **Avoid Overuse:** Be mindful not to overuse HOCs, as excessive nesting can make code harder to understand. Consider alternative patterns like Render Props or Hooks when appropriate.

Summary

Higher-Order Components (HOCs) are a powerful pattern in React for enhancing and reusing component logic. They allow you to abstract and share functionality between components, create reusable behavior, and compose multiple enhancements. While HOCs offer flexibility and code reuse, it's essential to use them judiciously and consider other patterns when appropriate.

Context API

The Context API is a feature in React that provides a way to share data between components without the need to pass props manually through each level of the component tree. It allows you to create a central store of data that can be accessed by any component in the tree, making it particularly useful for managing global state, themes, user authentication, and other application-wide data.

Using Context API

The Context API consists of three main parts:

1. **Context Object:** You create a context object using `React.createContext()`:

javascript
```
const MyContext = React.createContext();
```

2. **Provider Component:** You wrap a part of your component tree with a `Provider` component, which provides the context's value to its descendants:

javascript
```
<MyContext.Provider value={/* data you want to
share */}>
    {/* Your components here */}
  </MyContext.Provider>
```

3. **Consumer Component:** Any component in the tree can consume the context data using a `Consumer` component or the `useContext` Hook:

javascript
```
<MyContext.Consumer>
    {value => /* render something based on the
value */}
  </MyContext.Consumer>
```

  or

javascript
```
import { useContext } from 'react';

  const value = useContext(MyContext);
```

Example Usage

Here's a simplified example of how to use the Context API to manage and share a theme throughout your application:

javascript
```
import React, { createContext, useContext, useState
} from 'react';

// Create a context for the theme
const ThemeContext = createContext();

// Create a provider component
function ThemeProvider({ children }) {
  const [theme, setTheme] = useState('light');

  const toggleTheme = () => {
    setTheme(prevTheme => (prevTheme === 'light' ?
'dark' : 'light'));
  };

  return (
```

```
    <ThemeContext.Provider value={{ theme,
toggleTheme }}>
      {children}
    </ThemeContext.Provider>
  );
}

// Use a custom hook to consume the theme context
function useTheme() {
  return useContext(ThemeContext);
}

// Example usage in a component
function ThemeToggleButton() {
  const { theme, toggleTheme } = useTheme();

  return (
    <button onClick={toggleTheme}>
      Toggle Theme ({theme})
    </button>
  );
}
```

In this example, the `ThemeProvider` component wraps the application, providing access to the theme and a function to toggle it. The `useTheme` hook is used within components to access the theme context.

Benefits of the Context API

The Context API offers several advantages:

1. **Simplifies Prop Drilling:** It eliminates the need to pass props down through multiple levels of components, making the code cleaner and more maintainable.

2. **Global State Management:** You can use context to manage global state that multiple components need access to, such as authentication, user settings, or themes.

3. **Easier Theming:** Managing themes and styles across the entire application becomes more straightforward.

4. **Decouples Components:** Components consuming context data don't need to be tightly coupled to the components providing the data, promoting better component isolation and reusability.

Caveats and Considerations

While the Context API is powerful, there are some considerations to keep in mind:

1. **Performance**: Be cautious when using context for very large or frequently updating data, as it can lead to unnecessary re-renders of consuming components. Use memoization or other optimization techniques when needed.

2. **Overuse**: Avoid overusing context for every piece of data in your application, as it can make the component tree harder to understand and maintain. Use it for data that truly needs to be shared globally.

3. **Provider Placement**: Ensure that you place providers at an appropriate level in your component tree. Placing providers too high can lead to unnecessary re-renders, while placing them too low may limit the scope of the context.

Summary

The Context API in React is a powerful tool for sharing data between components without the need for extensive prop drilling. It simplifies global state management and makes it easier to manage themes, user authentication, and other application-wide data. However, it's essential to use the Context API judiciously and consider performance and component tree structure when implementing context in your application.

Testing in React

Testing is a critical aspect of building robust and maintainable React applications. It helps ensure that your components and application behave as expected, catch bugs early in development, and provide a safety net for future changes. React provides various tools and libraries for testing, making it easier to write tests for your components.

Types of Tests

In React testing, there are primarily two types of tests:

1. **Unit Tests:** Unit tests focus on testing individual components or functions in isolation. They ensure that each component behaves as expected when given specific inputs.

2. **Integration and End-to-End Tests:** Integration tests check how different parts of your application work together, while end-to-end tests verify the entire flow of the application, simulating user interactions. These tests provide confidence in the overall functionality.

Testing Libraries

Several libraries and tools are commonly used for testing React applications:

1. **React Testing Library:** React Testing Library is a popular library for testing React components. It emphasizes testing components from the user's perspective, making it easier to write tests that resemble real user interactions.

2. **Jest:** Jest is a JavaScript testing framework that is often used with React. It provides a robust testing environment, including assertion utilities, test runners, and mocking capabilities.

Writing Unit Tests with React Testing Library and Jest

Here's an example of how to write a unit test for a simple React component using React Testing Library and Jest:

javascript
```
import React from 'react';
import { render, fireEvent } from
'@testing-library/react';
import MyComponent from './MyComponent';

test('MyComponent renders and handles click', () =>
{
  // Render the component
  const { getByText } = render(<MyComponent />);

  // Check if the component renders properly
  const button = getByText('Click Me');
  expect(button).toBeInTheDocument();

  // Simulate a click event
  fireEvent.click(button);

  // Check if the component's state updates
correctly
  const result = getByText('Button clicked: 1');
  expect(result).toBeInTheDocument();
});
```

In this example, we render the `MyComponent` component, interact with it by clicking the button, and then assert that the component behaves as expected.

Integration and End-to-End Testing

For integration and end-to-end testing, you can use additional tools and libraries such as:

- **Cypress:** Cypress is a popular end-to-end testing framework that provides a comprehensive testing environment for web applications. It allows you to write tests that interact with your application as a user would.

- **React Testing Library with React Router:** When testing applications with client-side routing using libraries like React Router, you can use React Testing Library in combination with `react-router-dom` to simulate route changes and test navigation.

Best Practices

Here are some best practices for testing in React:

1. **Test Behavior, Not Implementation:** Focus on testing the behavior of your components, not their internal implementation details. This helps make tests more robust to refactoring.

2. **Isolate Components:** When writing unit tests, isolate the component being tested from its dependencies by using mocking or providing test-specific props.

3. **Test Edge Cases:** Be sure to test edge cases and boundary conditions to ensure your components handle various scenarios.

4. **Test User Interactions:** Write tests that simulate user interactions, such as clicking buttons, filling out forms, and navigating between screens.

5. **Continuous Integration:** Incorporate testing into your continuous integration (CI) pipeline to automatically run tests whenever code changes are pushed to your repository.

Summary

Testing is a crucial part of React application development. React provides tools like React Testing Library and Jest to make testing components and applications more accessible. By writing unit tests, integration tests, and end-to-end tests, you can ensure that your React application behaves correctly and remains maintainable as it grows.

Server-Side Rendering (SSR)

Server-Side Rendering (SSR) is a technique used in React and other modern web frameworks to render web pages on the server and send fully rendered HTML to the client, rather than relying on client-side JavaScript to generate and render the page. SSR offers several advantages, including improved performance, search engine optimization (SEO), and better user experience, especially on slower devices.

How SSR Works

In a typical client-side rendered (CSR) React application, JavaScript is responsible for fetching data, rendering components, and handling user interactions. In contrast, SSR shifts some of this work to the server:

1. **Request to the Server:** When a user requests a page, the server receives the request and starts generating the HTML for the requested page.

2. **Data Fetching:** The server may fetch data from various sources, such as APIs or databases, to populate the page with initial data.

3. **Rendering Components:** The server renders React components into HTML based on the requested route and data.

4. **Sending HTML to the Client:** The fully rendered HTML, along with any necessary CSS and JavaScript bundles, is sent to the client as a response.

5. **Hydration:** After the initial HTML is loaded and parsed by the browser, React takes over on the client side, rehydrating the components and making the page interactive.

Advantages of SSR

Server-Side Rendering offers several advantages:

1. **Improved Performance:** SSR can lead to faster initial page loads because the server sends fully rendered HTML, reducing the time required for JavaScript to load, parse, and execute.

2. **SEO Benefits:** Search engines can crawl and index SSR-generated pages more easily, improving the discoverability of your content.

3. **User Experience:** SSR can provide a better user experience on slower devices or poor network connections, as users can see and interact with content sooner.

4. **Content Sharing:** SSR improves content sharing on social media platforms by providing rich metadata in the initial HTML.

Challenges and Considerations

While SSR offers numerous benefits, it also presents some challenges and considerations:

1. **Complexity:** Implementing SSR can add complexity to your application, as it requires server-side rendering logic and often involves managing server-specific code.

2. **Server Load:** SSR can increase server load, especially for applications with high traffic, as the server must render pages for each request.

3. **Code Splitting:** Code splitting, a technique for optimizing JavaScript bundles, becomes more complex in SSR applications.

4. **Session Management:** Session management and user authentication may require special handling in SSR to ensure a seamless user experience.

Frameworks and Libraries for SSR

Several frameworks and libraries can help you implement SSR in React:

1. **Next.js:** Next.js is a popular React framework that simplifies SSR implementation, offering features like automatic code splitting, routing, and API routes.

2. **Gatsby:** Gatsby is a static site generator that uses React and GraphQL. It generates static HTML for pages at build time, providing the benefits of SSR with high performance.

3. **Express.js:** If you prefer a more custom solution, you can use a server framework like Express.js to implement SSR manually.

Choosing SSR vs. CSR

The decision to use SSR or CSR depends on your application's requirements. Consider SSR for:

- Content-heavy websites.
- SEO-sensitive applications.
- Better initial loading performance.
- Improved user experience on slower devices or networks.

However, CSR may be more suitable for:

- Highly interactive single-page applications (SPAs).
- Applications with complex client-side logic.
- Simpler content websites or web apps.

Summary

Server-Side Rendering (SSR) is a technique in React that involves rendering web pages on the server and sending fully rendered HTML to the client. SSR offers advantages like improved performance, SEO benefits, and better user experience. While it adds complexity to your application, frameworks like Next.js and Gatsby simplify SSR implementation, making it a valuable choice for many web applications.

React and Redux in Practice

React and Redux are often used together to manage state in complex React applications. Redux is a state management library that provides a predictable and centralized way to manage application state, while React is responsible for rendering the user interface. In practice, the combination of React and Redux can lead to scalable and maintainable applications.

Key Concepts of Redux

Before diving into practical usage, let's recap the key concepts of Redux:

1. **Store:** The store is a single, immutable object that holds the entire state of your application. It can be thought of as a centralized data repository.

2. **Actions:** Actions are plain JavaScript objects that describe changes to the state. They must have a `type` property and can carry additional data.

3. **Reducers:** Reducers are pure functions that specify how the application's state should change in response to actions. They take the current state and an action as input and return the new state.

4. **Dispatch:** Dispatch is a method provided by Redux to send actions to the store. When an action is dispatched, it triggers a state change.

5. **Selectors:** Selectors are functions that allow you to access specific pieces of data from the store. They can help simplify access to state data in your components.

Practical Usage of React and Redux

Here's a high-level overview of how React and Redux are used together in practice:

1. **Setting Up Redux:**
   - Install Redux and related libraries (e.g., `redux`, `react-redux`).
   - Create a Redux store, combining reducers using `combineReducers`.
   - Set up the Redux store in your application by wrapping it with the `Provider` component from `react-redux`.

2. **Defining Actions and Reducers:**
   - Define action types as constants to maintain consistency.
   - Create action creators, functions that return action objects.
   - Write reducers for each slice of your application's state.

3. **Dispatching Actions:**
   - In your React components, use the `useDispatch` hook to access the `dispatch` function.
   - Dispatch actions when specific events occur, such as user interactions or data fetching.

4. **Accessing State:**
   - Use the `useSelector` hook to access data from the Redux store in your components.
   - Selectors can help extract specific pieces of state for rendering.

5. **Updating the UI:**
   - When actions are dispatched and the state changes, React components re-render to reflect the updated data.

6. **Middleware (Optional):**
   - You can use middleware like `redux-thunk` or `redux-saga` to handle asynchronous actions, side effects, and more complex logic.

7. **Selectors and Memoization:**

- Optimize component performance by using memoization techniques with selectors to prevent unnecessary re-renders.

8. Testing:
- Write unit tests for your action creators, reducers, and selectors to ensure they work as expected.
- Use tools like Jest and testing utilities provided by Redux for testing.

Best Practices

When working with React and Redux, consider the following best practices:

1. **Single Source of Truth:** Maintain a single Redux store that contains the entire application state.

2. **Keep Reducers Pure:** Reducers should be pure functions without side effects. They should not modify the state directly.

3. **Use Selectors:** Use selectors to access specific pieces of state and avoid direct access to the store.

4. **Normalize State:** Consider normalizing complex state structures to simplify data management.

5. **Middleware for Side Effects:** Use middleware to handle asynchronous actions and side effects.

6. **Component Structure:** Organize your components into presentational and container components. Presentational components focus on rendering, while container components connect to Redux and manage data.

Summary

React and Redux are a powerful combination for building complex and scalable applications. Redux provides a centralized and predictable way to manage state, while React takes care of rendering the user interface. By following best practices and structuring your application effectively, you can create maintainable and efficient applications with these technologies.

Building Real-World Applications

Building a To-Do List Application

A To-Do List application is a classic example of a simple web application that can be built using React. It provides an excellent opportunity to practice fundamental React concepts and state management. In this chapter, we'll walk through the steps to build a basic To-Do List application.

Project Setup

Before you start building the To-Do List application, make sure you have React installed and set up in your development environment. You can use tools like Create React App to quickly create a new React project or set up your project manually.

Key Features of the To-Do List Application

Here are the key features that we'll implement in the To-Do List application:

1. **Add To-Do Items:** Users can add new tasks to the list.

2. **Mark Tasks as Completed:** Users can mark tasks as completed or uncompleted by clicking on them.

3. **Delete Tasks:** Users can delete tasks from the list.

4. **Filter Tasks:** Users can filter tasks to view all tasks, completed tasks, or active tasks.

Component Structure

Here's the basic component structure for our To-Do List application:

1. `App.js`: The main component that holds the state and renders other components.
2. `TodoForm.js`: A component for adding new tasks.
3. `TodoList.js`: A component for displaying the list of tasks.
4. `TodoItem.js`: A component for rendering individual tasks.
5. `FilterButtons.js`: A component for filtering tasks.

State Management

In the `App.js` component, we'll manage the application's state using React's built-in state management. The state will consist of an array of to-do items, where each item has a description and a `completed` flag.

javascript

```javascript
// App.js
import React, { useState } from 'react';
import TodoForm from './TodoForm';
import TodoList from './TodoList';
import FilterButtons from './FilterButtons';

function App() {
  const [todos, setTodos] = useState([]);
  const [filter, setFilter] = useState('All');

  // Function to add a new task
  const addTodo = (text) => {
    const newTodo = { text, completed: false };
    setTodos([...todos, newTodo]);
  };
```

```
// Function to toggle task completion
const toggleTodo = (index) => {
  const updatedTodos = [...todos];
  updatedTodos[index].completed =
!updatedTodos[index].completed;
  setTodos(updatedTodos);
};

// Function to delete a task
const deleteTodo = (index) => {
  const updatedTodos = todos.filter((_, i) => i
!== index);
  setTodos(updatedTodos);
};

return (
  <div className="App">
    <h1>My To-Do List</h1>
    <TodoForm addTodo={addTodo} />
    <FilterButtons setFilter={setFilter} />
    <TodoList
      todos={todos}
      filter={filter}
      toggleTodo={toggleTodo}
      deleteTodo={deleteTodo}
    />
  </div>
);
}

export default App;
```

TodoForm Component

The `TodoForm` component allows users to input new tasks and add them to the list when submitted.

javascript
```javascript
// TodoForm.js
import React, { useState } from 'react';

function TodoForm({ addTodo }) {
  const [text, setText] = useState('');

  const handleSubmit = (e) => {
    e.preventDefault();
    if (text.trim() !== '') {
      addTodo(text);
      setText('');
    }
  };

  return (
    <form onSubmit={handleSubmit}>
      <input
        type="text"
        placeholder="Add a new task..."
        value={text}
        onChange={(e) => setText(e.target.value)}
      />
      <button type="submit">Add</button>
    </form>
  );
}

export default TodoForm;
```

TodoList Component

The `TodoList` component displays the list of tasks and handles filtering.

javascript

```javascript
// TodoList.js
import React from 'react';
import TodoItem from './TodoItem';

function TodoList({ todos, filter, toggleTodo,
deleteTodo }) {
  const filteredTodos = filter === 'All'
    ? todos
    : filter === 'Completed'
    ? todos.filter(todo => todo.completed)
    : todos.filter(todo => !todo.completed);

  return (
    <ul className='ToDoList'>
      {filteredTodos.map((todo, index) => (
        <TodoItem
          key={index}
          todo={todo}
          index={index}
          toggleTodo={toggleTodo}
          deleteTodo={deleteTodo}
        />
      ))}
    </ul>
  );
}

export default TodoList;
```

TodoItem Component

The `TodoItem` component renders individual tasks and handles task completion and deletion.

javascript
```javascript
// TodoItem.js
import React from 'react';

function TodoItem({ todo, index, toggleTodo,
deleteTodo }) {
  return (
    <li className="ToDoItem">
      <input
        type="checkbox"
        checked={todo.completed}
        onChange={() => toggleTodo(index)}
      />
      <span className={todo.completed ? 'completed'
: ''}>{todo.text}</span>
      <button className="DeleteButton" onClick={()
=> deleteTodo(index)}>Delete</button>
    </li>
  );
}

export default TodoItem;
```

FilterButtons Component

The `FilterButtons` component provides buttons to filter tasks.

javascript
```javascript
// FilterButtons.js
import React from 'react';

function FilterButtons({ setFilter }) {
  return (
    <div className="filter-buttons">
      <button onClick={() =>
setFilter('All')}>All</button>
```

```
        <button onClick={() =>
setFilter('Active')}>Active</button>
        <button onClick={() =>
setFilter('Completed')}>Completed</button>
    </div>
  );
}

export default FilterButtons;
```

Certainly! Below, I'll provide you with some styling and testing examples for the To-Do List Application that we created using React. I'll start with styling examples and then move on to testing.

Styling

Styling in React applications can be achieved through CSS, CSS-in-JS libraries like Styled Components, or CSS frameworks like Bootstrap. I'll provide an example using simple CSS:

css
```
/* styles.css */
/* Style the overall app container */
.App {
  text-align: center;
  font-family: Arial, sans-serif;
  background-color: #f0f0f0;
  padding: 20px;
}

/* Style the To-Do List container */
.ToDoList {
  max-width: 400px;
  margin: 0 auto;
  background-color: white;
  border: 1px solid #ccc;
```

```css
  padding: 20px;
  box-shadow: 0px 0px 5px rgba(0, 0, 0, 0.2);
}

/* Style individual to-do items */
.ToDoItem {
  display: flex;
  justify-content: space-between;
  align-items: center;
  margin-bottom: 10px;
  padding: 10px;
  background-color: #fff;
  border: 1px solid #ddd;
  border-radius: 4px;
}

/* Style the "Complete" button */
.CompleteButton {
  background-color: #5cb85c;
  color: white;
  border: none;
  padding: 5px 10px;
  cursor: pointer;
  border-radius: 4px;
}

/* Style the "Delete" button */
.DeleteButton {
  background-color: #d9534f;
  color: white;
  border: none;
  padding: 5px 10px;
  cursor: pointer;
  border-radius: 4px;
}

/* Style the input for adding new tasks */
.NewTaskInput {
  width: 100%;
```

```
  padding: 10px;
  border: 1px solid #ccc;
  border-radius: 4px;
}
```

You can include this CSS file in your React application and apply the styles to the respective components. For example, you can add `className="ToDoList"` to the `ToDoList` component to apply the styling defined in the `.ToDoList` CSS class.

Testing

Testing is a critical part of software development to ensure that your application functions as expected. Let's use Jest and React Testing Library for testing our To-Do List Application. First, make sure you have these libraries installed:

bash
```
npm install --save jest @testing-library/react
@testing-library/jest-dom
```

Now, let's create a test file for your application. You can create a `App.test.js` file:

javascript
```
// App.test.js

import React from 'react';
import { render, fireEvent } from
'@testing-library/react';
import App from './App';

test('renders to-do items correctly', () => {
  const { getByText } = render(<App />);
```

```
  // Assert that the initial to-do item is rendered
  const initialItem = getByText('Buy groceries');
  expect(initialItem).toBeInTheDocument();
});

test('adds a new to-do item', () => {
  const { getByPlaceholderText, getByText } =
render(<App />);
  const input = getByPlaceholderText('Add a new
task...');
  const addButton = getByText('Add');

  // Simulate user input and click
  fireEvent.change(input, { target: { value: 'Walk
the dog' } });
  fireEvent.click(addButton);

  // Assert that the new to-do item is added
  const newToDoItem = getByText('Walk the dog');
  expect(newToDoItem).toBeInTheDocument();
});

test('completes a to-do item', () => {
  const { getByText } = render(<App />);
  const completeButton = getByText('Complete');

  // Simulate clicking the "Complete" button
  fireEvent.click(completeButton);

  // Assert that the to-do item is marked as
completed
  expect(completeButton).toHaveClass('completed');
});

test('deletes a to-do item', () => {
  const { getByText } = render(<App />);
  const deleteButton = getByText('Delete');

  // Simulate clicking the "Delete" button
```

```
fireEvent.click(deleteButton);

// Assert that the to-do item is removed
expect(deleteButton).not.toBeInTheDocument();
});
```

These test cases cover basic functionality such as rendering, adding, completing, and deleting to-do items. You can expand and customize the tests to match the specific behavior of your To-Do List Application.

Remember to adjust the import statements and component names to match your project structure. To run the tests, use the `npm test` command.

Deployment

Once your To-Do List application is complete and tested, you can deploy it to a hosting service of your choice, such as Netlify, Vercel, or GitHub Pages, to make it accessible online.

This example provides a basic structure for building a To-Do List application in React. You can further customize and expand the functionality to create a more feature-rich application.

Developing a Chat Application

Developing a chat application is a complex task that often involves real-time communication and state management. I'll provide you with a simplified example of a chat application using React and Firebase for real-time functionality. This example won't cover every aspect of a complete chat application, but it will get you started.

Set Up Firebase

First, you need to set up Firebase for real-time database functionality. Go to the Firebase Console (https://console.firebase.google.com/) and create a new project. Once your project is created, click on "Database" in the left sidebar and set up a Realtime Database.

Next, configure Firebase in your React application by installing the Firebase SDK:

bash
```
npm install firebase
```

Then, initialize Firebase in your project:

jsx
```
// firebase.js

import firebase from 'firebase/app';
import 'firebase/database';

const firebaseConfig = {
  apiKey: 'YOUR_API_KEY',
  authDomain: 'YOUR_AUTH_DOMAIN',
  databaseURL: 'YOUR_DATABASE_URL',
  projectId: 'YOUR_PROJECT_ID',
  storageBucket: 'YOUR_STORAGE_BUCKET',
  messagingSenderId: 'YOUR_MESSAGING_SENDER_ID',
```

```
  appId: 'YOUR_APP_ID',
};

firebase.initializeApp(firebaseConfig);

export default firebase;
```

Replace the placeholder values with your Firebase project configuration.

Create the Chat Component

Now, let's create a Chat component in your React application. This component will handle sending and displaying messages.

jsx
```
import React, { useState, useEffect } from 'react';
import firebase from './firebase';

function Chat() {
  const [message, setMessage] = useState('');
  const [messages, setMessages] = useState([]);
  const db = firebase.database();

  // Load initial messages from Firebase
  useEffect(() => {
    const messagesRef = db.ref('messages');
    messagesRef.on('value', (snapshot) => {
      const messagesData = snapshot.val() || {};
      const messagesList =
Object.values(messagesData);
      setMessages(messagesList);
    });
  }, []);

  const handleSendMessage = () => {
    if (message.trim() !== '') {
```

```
      const messageObj = {
        text: message,
        timestamp:
firebase.database.ServerValue.TIMESTAMP,
      };
      db.ref('messages').push(messageObj);
      setMessage('');
    }
  };

  return (
    <div>
      <h2>Chat Application</h2>
      <div className="chat-box">
        <div className="message-list">
          {messages.map((msg, index) => (
            <div key={index} className="message">
              {msg.text}
            </div>
          ))}
        </div>
        <div className="message-input">
          <input
            type="text"
            placeholder="Type your message..."
            value={message}
            onChange={(e) =>
setMessage(e.target.value)}
          />
          <button
onClick={handleSendMessage}>Send</button>
        </div>
      </div>
    </div>
  );
}

export default Chat;
```

In this code:

- We initialize the Firebase database and set up the state to store messages.
- The `useEffect` hook loads initial messages from Firebase when the component mounts.
- The `handleSendMessage` function sends a new message to Firebase when the "Send" button is clicked.

Remember that this is a simplified example, and a production-ready chat application would require more features, such as user authentication, message storage, and real-time updates. Additionally, you'd need to handle security rules in Firebase to protect your data.

Styling

Certainly! Here's a simple CSS stylesheet to style the chat application. You can include this CSS in your project to apply the specified styles to the Chat component:

css
```css
/* styles.css */

/* Overall container for the chat application */
.chat-container {
  display: flex;
  flex-direction: column;
  align-items: center;
  justify-content: center;
  height: 100vh;
  background-color: #f0f0f0;
}

/* Chat box */
.chat-box {
  background-color: #fff;
  border: 1px solid #ddd;
```

```css
  border-radius: 4px;
  width: 300px;
  padding: 20px;
  box-shadow: 0px 0px 5px rgba(0, 0, 0, 0.2);
}

/* Message list */
.message-list {
  max-height: 300px;
  overflow-y: scroll;
}

/* Individual message */
.message {
  background-color: #f3f3f3;
  border: 1px solid #ddd;
  border-radius: 4px;
  padding: 10px;
  margin-bottom: 10px;
}

/* Message input area */
.message-input {
  display: flex;
  justify-content: space-between;
  align-items: center;
  margin-top: 20px;
}

/* Message input field */
.message-input input {
  flex: 1;
  padding: 10px;
  border: 1px solid #ddd;
  border-radius: 4px;
}

/* Send button */
.message-input button {
```

```
  background-color: #007bff;
  color: #fff;
  border: none;
  border-radius: 4px;
  padding: 10px 20px;
  cursor: pointer;
}

/* Send button hover effect */
.message-input button:hover {
  background-color: #0056b3;
}
```

To apply these styles to your Chat component, make sure you import this CSS file into the component where you render the Chat component. You can do this by adding the following line at the top of your Chat.js file:

jsx
```
import './styles.css';
```

This will link the CSS styles to your Chat component, and the styles will be applied when you render the component. Feel free to adjust the styles as needed to match your design preferences.

Testing

Testing a chat application can be quite complex, especially when dealing with real-time functionality and databases like Firebase. To simplify the process, I'll provide you with a basic example of testing the `Chat` component using Jest and React Testing Library for rendering and user interaction tests.

First, make sure you have Jest and React Testing Library installed:

bash

```
npm install --save jest @testing-library/react
@testing-library/jest-dom
```

Here's a testing example for the `Chat` component:

jsx

```jsx
// Chat.test.js

import React from 'react';
import { render, fireEvent } from
'@testing-library/react';
import Chat from './Chat'; // Import your Chat
component

test('renders chat component correctly', () => {
  const { getByText, getByPlaceholderText } =
render(<Chat />);

  // Assert that the chat title is displayed
  const chatTitle = getByText('Chat Application');
  expect(chatTitle).toBeInTheDocument();

  // Assert that the message input field and send
button are displayed
  const messageInput = getByPlaceholderText('Type
your message...');
  expect(messageInput).toBeInTheDocument();
  const sendButton = getByText('Send');
  expect(sendButton).toBeInTheDocument();
});

test('adds a new message when Send button is
clicked', () => {
  const { getByPlaceholderText, getByText,
getByTestId } = render(<Chat />);

  // Find the input field and the send button
```

```
  const messageInput = getByPlaceholderText('Type
your message...');
  const sendButton = getByText('Send');

  // Type a message and click the send button
  fireEvent.change(messageInput, { target: { value:
'Hello, Chat!' } });
  fireEvent.click(sendButton);

  // Assert that the new message is displayed
  const newMessage = getByText('Hello, Chat!');
  expect(newMessage).toBeInTheDocument();

  // You can also test other conditions like
clearing the input field
  expect(messageInput.value).toBe('');
});

// You can add more tests for other features as
needed
```

In this example, we have two basic tests:

1. The first test checks if the Chat component renders correctly by asserting the presence of the chat title, message input field, and send button.

2. The second test simulates typing a message and clicking the send button, then asserts that the new message is displayed.

Please note that this is a basic testing example, and a production chat application would require more extensive testing, especially for real-time and database interactions. Additionally, you may consider using a testing library specifically designed for Firebase, such as `firebase-functions-test`, for more comprehensive testing of Firebase-related functionality.

Deployment

Deploying a real-time chat application involves deploying both the frontend and backend components. You'll need a server to handle WebSocket communication and store message history.

Please note that this is a simplified example, and building a full-featured chat application involves more complex functionality, including user authentication, message storage, and scalability considerations. Additionally, you'd need to create a backend server to manage WebSocket connections and handle messages.

Performance Optimization

Profiling React Applications

Profiling involves measuring the performance of your React components to identify areas that need optimization. React provides a built-in tool called the React Profiler that allows you to record and analyze component rendering times.

Here's how you can use the React Profiler:

1. **Import React Profiler:**

javascript
```
import { unstable_trace as trace } from
'scheduler/tracing';
import React from 'react';
```

2. **Wrap Components with Profiler:**

You can wrap your components with the `<Profiler>` component to measure their rendering performance. The Profiler requires two props: `id` (a unique identifier for the profiler) and `onRender` (a callback function that receives timing information).

javascript
```
<React.Profiler id="myComponent"
onRender={callback}>
    <MyComponent />
</React.Profiler>
```

3. **Analyze Profiler Results:**

After running your application with profiling enabled, you can inspect the results in the browser's DevTools. The profiler will show you which components are rendering, how often they render, and how long rendering takes.

Optimizing Components

Once you've identified performance bottlenecks using profiling, you can apply various optimization techniques to improve your components' efficiency:

1. **Memoization with React.memo:**

Use the `React.memo` higher-order component to memoize functional components and prevent unnecessary re-renders. This can be especially useful for optimizing pure components that depend on props.

javascript
```javascript
const MyMemoizedComponent =
React.memo(MyComponent);
```

2. **Pure Components:**

In class components, you can extend `React.PureComponent` to automatically implement shallow prop and state comparison. This can help prevent re-renders when props or state haven't changed.

javascript
```javascript
class MyPureComponent extends React.PureComponent
{
  // ...
}
```

3. Use shouldComponentUpdate:

In class components, you can manually implement the
`shouldComponentUpdate` method to specify when a component
should update based on custom logic.

javascript
```
shouldComponentUpdate(nextProps, nextState) {
    // Return true or false based on your custom
comparison logic.
  }
```

4. Memoization with useMemo and useCallback:

In functional components, you can use the `useMemo` hook to
memoize computed values and the `useCallback` hook to memoize
functions. This can reduce unnecessary calculations and function
recreations.

javascript
```
const memoizedValue = useMemo(() =>
computeValue(dep1, dep2), [dep1, dep2]);
    const memoizedCallback = useCallback(() =>
doSomething(dep), [dep]);
```

5. Lazy Loading and Code Splitting:

Consider lazy loading components and using code splitting techniques
to load only the necessary code when it's needed. This can significantly
improve initial load times and reduce the bundle size.

javascript
```
import { lazy, Suspense } from 'react';

const LazyComponent = lazy(() =>
import('./LazyComponent'));
```

6. **Virtualization:**

For long lists or tables, consider using virtualization libraries like `react-virtualized` or `react-window` to render only the visible items, reducing the DOM size and improving rendering performance.

These are just a few optimization techniques you can apply to your React components. The specific optimizations you choose will depend on your application's requirements and the results of profiling. Regularly profiling and optimizing your components can lead to a more responsive and efficient React application.

Memoization

Memoization is a technique that stores the results of expensive function calls and returns the cached result when the same inputs occur again. This can significantly improve the performance of functions or components that are computationally expensive or have frequent re-renders.

In the context of React, memoization is often used to optimize functional components and hooks.

Memoization with React.memo

`React.memo` is a built-in React feature that allows you to memoize functional components. When you wrap a component with `React.memo`, it will only re-render if its props change. This can prevent unnecessary re-renders and improve the performance of your application.

Here's how to use `React.memo`:

javascript
```javascript
import React from 'react';

const MyComponent = ({ prop1, prop2 }) => {
  // Your component logic here
};

export default React.memo(MyComponent);
```

In the code above, `MyComponent` will only re-render if `prop1` or `prop2` change. If the props remain the same, the cached result of the previous render will be used.

Memoization with useMemo and useCallback

In functional components, you can use the `useMemo` and `useCallback` hooks to memoize values and functions, respectively.

- **useMemo**: Use this hook to memoize the result of a computation based on one or more dependencies. It takes a function that performs the computation and an array of dependencies. The memoized value is recalculated only when one of the dependencies changes.

javascript
```
const memoizedValue = useMemo(() =>
computeValue(prop1, prop2), [prop1, prop2]);
```

- **useCallback**: Use this hook to memoize a function. It takes a function and an array of dependencies. The memoized function is created only when one of the dependencies changes.

javascript
```
const memoizedFunction = useCallback(() =>
doSomething(prop), [prop]);
```

By using `useMemo` and `useCallback`, you can prevent unnecessary recalculations and function recreations, which can improve the performance of your components.

When to Use Memoization

You should consider using memoization in the following scenarios:

1. When a component or function has expensive calculations that don't need to be repeated on every render.

2. When a component relies on props that don't change frequently.

3. When you want to optimize the performance of a component that renders frequently.

By applying memoization strategically in your React application, you can reduce unnecessary computation and re-renders, leading to a more efficient and responsive user interface.

Code splitting

Code splitting is a technique used to improve the performance of web applications by breaking the codebase into smaller, more manageable chunks. This allows you to load only the code that is needed for a particular route or feature, reducing initial loading times and improving the user experience.

Why Code Splitting?

Code splitting is important for several reasons:

1. **Faster Initial Load Times:** Loading a large JavaScript bundle can significantly slow down the initial loading of your application. Code splitting reduces the size of the initial bundle, leading to faster load times.

2. **Improved User Experience:** Users get a faster, more responsive experience because they don't have to wait for the entire application to load.

3. **Optimized Resource Usage:** Only the code necessary for a particular route or feature is loaded, reducing the memory and CPU usage.

How to Implement Code Splitting in React

React provides several mechanisms for implementing code splitting:

1. Dynamic Imports with import()

You can use dynamic imports to load modules asynchronously. This is typically done with the `import()` function, which returns a promise that resolves to the module.

javascript
```javascript
const LazyComponent = React.lazy(() =>
import('./LazyComponent'));
```

This is particularly useful for lazy loading components, where the component is only loaded when it's needed.

2. React.lazy and Suspense

React's `React.lazy` function allows you to dynamically import a component and use it with the `Suspense` component to display a fallback while the component is loading.

javascript
```javascript
import React, { lazy, Suspense } from 'react';

const LazyComponent = lazy(() =>
import('./LazyComponent'));

function App() {
  return (
    <div>
      <Suspense fallback={<div>Loading...</div>}>
        <LazyComponent />
      </Suspense>
    </div>
  );
}
```

3. Route-Based Code Splitting

You can also use code splitting based on routes. Popular routing libraries like React Router offer built-in support for lazy loading components on a per-route basis.

javascript
```
const Home = React.lazy(() => import('./Home'));
const About = React.lazy(() =>
import('./About'));

<Switch>
  <Route path="/" exact component={Home} />
  <Route path="/about" component={About} />
</Switch>
```

4. Webpack SplitChunksPlugin

If you're using Webpack as your bundler, you can use the `SplitChunksPlugin` to automatically split your code into chunks. It analyzes your dependencies and creates separate bundles for shared code.

javascript
```
// webpack.config.js
optimization: {
  splitChunks: {
    chunks: 'all',
  },
},
```

Best Practices for Code Splitting

- Split your code into logical chunks, such as routes or feature modules.
- Use code splitting for large dependencies or components that are not needed immediately.

- Test your application thoroughly after implementing code splitting to ensure that all dependencies are loaded correctly.
- Monitor your application's performance to identify any performance bottlenecks or issues.

By implementing code splitting in your React application, you can significantly improve its performance, reduce initial loading times, and provide users with a faster and more responsive experience.

Lazy Loading

Lazy loading is a technique used to improve the performance of web applications by deferring the loading of non-essential resources until they are actually needed. This technique is especially useful for optimizing the loading of images, scripts, and other assets in a web page.

Why Lazy Loading?

Lazy loading is important for several reasons:

1. **Faster Initial Page Load:** By delaying the loading of non-essential resources, you can reduce the initial page load time, allowing users to access the core content of your application more quickly.

2. **Improved User Experience:** Users can start interacting with your application sooner, leading to a better overall user experience.

3. **Optimized Resource Usage:** Lazy loading can help conserve bandwidth and reduce server load by only requesting resources when they are actually needed.

How to Implement Lazy Loading in React

Lazy loading can be implemented in React for various types of resources, such as images, components, and external libraries. Here are some ways to implement lazy loading in a React application:

1. **Lazy Loading Images:**

You can use the `loading` attribute for images to enable lazy loading:

jsx

```
<img
  src="image.jpg"
  alt="Lazy Loaded Image"
  loading="lazy"
/>
```

This tells the browser to load the image only when it's about to enter the viewport.

2. Lazy Loading Components:

React provides a built-in mechanism for lazy loading components using the `React.lazy` function and `Suspense`:

```jsx
import React, { lazy, Suspense } from 'react';

const LazyComponent = lazy(() =>
import('./LazyComponent'));

function App() {
  return (
    <div>
      <Suspense fallback={<div>Loading...</div>}>
        <LazyComponent />
      </Suspense>
    </div>
  );
}
```

With this approach, the `LazyComponent` will be loaded only when it's rendered.

3. Lazy Loading External Libraries:

You can use dynamic imports to load external libraries lazily:

jsx
```jsx
import('external-library').then((externalModule)
=> {
    // Use the external module when it's loaded
});
```

This is particularly useful for large third-party libraries that are not needed immediately on page load.

Best Practices for Lazy Loading

- Identify resources that are not immediately required for the initial view of your application.
- Prioritize lazy loading for resources that are below the fold (i.e., not visible without scrolling) or not essential for the core functionality.
- Be mindful of the user experience. Ensure that the lazy-loaded content is loaded quickly when it's requested.

By implementing lazy loading in your React application, you can improve the overall performance, reduce initial page load times, and provide users with a faster and more efficient experience.

Server-Side Rendering (SSR)

Server-Side Rendering (SSR) is a performance optimization technique used in web development to improve the initial load time and search engine optimization (SEO) of web applications. In this chapter you'll learn about how to implement SSR in a React application to achieve faster page loads and better SEO.

What is Server-Side Rendering (SSR)?

In traditional client-side rendering (CSR), the web browser downloads a minimal HTML page and then relies on JavaScript to render the rest of the page. This means that users often see a blank or loading screen while the JavaScript is being downloaded and executed.

Server-Side Rendering (SSR) shifts some of the rendering work from the client-side (browser) to the server-side (web server). With SSR, the server generates the initial HTML for a page and sends it to the browser. This allows the browser to display the content much faster, as it doesn't have to wait for JavaScript to complete before rendering.

Benefits of SSR:

1. **Faster Initial Load:** SSR provides a faster initial load experience for users since they receive a fully rendered HTML page from the server.

2. **SEO Improvements:** Search engines can crawl and index the content of SSR-rendered pages more easily, leading to better SEO rankings.

3. **Improved User Experience:** Users see content more quickly, resulting in a better overall user experience.

Implementing SSR in React:

To implement SSR in a React application, you can use frameworks like Next.js or custom solutions with libraries like React Server Components. Here's a simplified overview of how SSR works with Next.js:

1. Create a Next.js Application:

Start by creating a Next.js application using the `create-next-app` command or by setting up a Next.js project manually.

2. Create Pages:

In Next.js, pages are automatically associated with routes. Create the pages for your application using the `pages` directory structure.

3. Implement getServerSideProps:

Use the `getServerSideProps` function in your page components to fetch data from APIs or databases and pass it as props to the page. This function runs on the server for SSR.

```jsx
export async function getServerSideProps(context)
{
  // Fetch data from an API or database
  const data = await fetchData();

  return {
    props: { data },
  };
}
```

4. Use the next CLI:

Start the development server with `next dev`, and for production, use `next build` and `next start` to build and serve your SSR application.

Limitations and Considerations:

- SSR may increase server load, especially for frequently accessed pages, so ensure that your server infrastructure can handle the additional load.
- Components that rely heavily on client-side JavaScript for interactivity may require additional work to function properly with SSR.
- Be mindful of data fetching and authentication when using SSR, as it may differ from client-side data fetching.

Server-Side Rendering can be a powerful tool for optimizing React applications, especially for content-heavy websites and applications where SEO and initial load times are critical. By moving some rendering work to the server, you can provide a better experience for users and search engines.

Best Practices and Tips

Code Quality and Style

Code quality and style are essential aspects of building maintainable, readable, and efficient React applications. Here's a summary of the key points regarding code quality and style in React:

1. Consistent Code Style:

- **Formatting:** Use a consistent code formatter like Prettier to enforce a unified code style across your project. Configure your IDE or text editor to automatically format code on save.

- **Linting:** Utilize ESLint with popular configurations (e.g., Airbnb, Standard) to catch and fix code issues, enforce coding standards, and ensure consistency.

2. Follow React Best Practices:

- **Component Structure:** Organize your components in a structured manner. Keep them focused and single-responsibility. Use functional components when possible.

- **Props:** Ensure that component props are well-documented with PropTypes or TypeScript to maintain type safety and provide clear expectations for component usage.

- **State Management:** Follow best practices for state management, whether using React's built-in state, Context API, Redux, or other libraries. Avoid unnecessary state duplication.

- **Lifecycle Methods:** Be aware of lifecycle methods in class components and use them appropriately. For functional components, leverage the useEffect hook for side effects.

3. Maintainable and Readable Code:

- **Descriptive Variable and Function Names:** Use clear and meaningful variable and function names to enhance code readability. Avoid cryptic or overly abbreviated names.

- **Comments and Documentation:** Document complex logic, functions, and components using comments. Provide context and explanations where needed but avoid redundant comments.

- **Modularization:** Break down your application into smaller, reusable components and modules. Keep components as independent as possible.

4. Performance Optimization:

- **Memoization:** Use memoization techniques to prevent unnecessary re-renders of components and expensive computations. Utilize React.memo, useMemo, and useCallback.

- **Code Splitting:** Implement code splitting to load only the necessary code for each route or feature, improving initial loading times.

- **Lazy Loading:** Lazy load components, images, and external dependencies to reduce initial page load times and improve user experience.

5. Testing and Quality Assurance:

- **Unit Testing:** Write unit tests for your React components and functions using testing libraries like Jest and React Testing Library. Test critical functionality and edge cases.

- **Integration Testing:** Perform integration testing to ensure that different parts of your application work together correctly.

6. Code Review and Collaboration:

- **Code Reviews:** Conduct code reviews to maintain code quality and share knowledge among team members. Use code review tools and checklists to ensure consistency.

- **Version Control:** Use version control systems (e.g., Git) effectively, following best practices for branching, merging, and commit messages.

7. Maintain a Clean Git History:

- **Commit Frequently:** Make small, focused commits that address specific issues or features. Avoid large, monolithic commits.

- **Use Meaningful Commit Messages:** Write clear and descriptive commit messages that explain the purpose and context of the changes.

8. Continuous Integration (CI) and Continuous Deployment (CD):

- **CI/CD Pipeline:** Set up a CI/CD pipeline to automate code testing, build processes, and deployment. This ensures that code quality is maintained throughout the development lifecycle.

9. Documentation:

 - **Project Documentation:** Maintain project documentation that includes setup instructions, architecture diagrams, and explanations of major components and decisions.

10. Stay Updated:

 - **React and Libraries:** Keep your React version and related libraries up to date to benefit from performance improvements and security updates.

Maintaining high code quality and adhering to consistent coding styles are crucial for the long-term success and maintainability of your React applications. By following these best practices, your team can write clean, efficient, and maintainable code, making it easier to collaborate and scale your projects.

Debugging React Applications

Debugging is an essential skill for React developers, and it plays a crucial role in identifying and fixing issues in your applications. Here's a summary of the key points related to debugging React applications:

1. Use Developer Tools:

Modern web browsers come equipped with powerful developer tools that provide various debugging features specifically designed for React applications. You can access these tools by pressing F12 or right-clicking and selecting "Inspect" in your browser.

2. React DevTools:

React DevTools is a browser extension available for Chrome, Firefox, and other browsers. It's an indispensable tool for debugging React applications as it provides insights into your component hierarchy, props, state, and more. You can install React DevTools as an extension and then access it through your browser's developer tools.

3. Debugging Components:

 - **Inspect Component Hierarchy:** In React DevTools, you can inspect the component hierarchy, view component props and state, and identify the relationships between components.

 - **Highlight Updates:** React DevTools can highlight components that re-render, making it easier to identify performance bottlenecks and unnecessary renders.

- **State and Props Inspection:** Inspect the values of component state and props in real-time to understand how data flows through your application.

4. Console Debugging:

- **Console Logging:** Use `console.log()`, `console.warn()`, and `console.error()` statements strategically to log information about your application's state and execution flow.

- **Console Grouping:** Group related log messages using `console.group()` and `console.groupEnd()` to create a more organized and readable console output.

5. Debugging Tools for Hooks:

- **React DevTools for Hooks:** React DevTools provides dedicated support for debugging React Hooks, allowing you to inspect the state of hooks, their order, and dependencies.

6. Error Boundaries:

- **Use Error Boundaries:** Implement error boundaries in your application to gracefully handle errors and prevent them from crashing your entire app. You can use `componentDidCatch` in class components and the `ErrorBoundary` component in functional components.

- **Error Messages:** Display user-friendly error messages when an error boundary catches an error to provide clear feedback to users.

7. Testing and Test Debugging:

- **Unit Testing:** Write unit tests for your components and functions using testing libraries like Jest and React Testing Library. Debug test failures by inspecting the test runner's output and using debugging tools.

- **Integration Testing:** For more complex interactions between components, write integration tests to identify issues that may not be apparent during unit testing.

8. Chrome DevTools Tips:

- **Conditional Breakpoints:** Set conditional breakpoints in Chrome DevTools to pause code execution when specific conditions are met.

- **Step Through Code:** Use the step into, step over, and step out of functions options to navigate through your code during debugging.

- **Watch Expressions:** Add watch expressions to keep an eye on specific variables or values as they change.

9. Debugging in Production:

- **Source Maps:** Ensure that you generate and include source maps in your production build. Source maps allow you to debug minified and transpiled code in the browser's developer tools.

Debugging is a skill that improves with practice. By becoming proficient in debugging React applications, you can effectively identify and resolve issues, leading to more robust and reliable web applications.

Security Considerations

Ensuring the security of your application is crucial, as vulnerabilities can lead to data breaches, unauthorized access, and other security incidents. Here's a summary of the key security considerations for React applications:

1. Input Validation and Sanitization:

- Always validate and sanitize user inputs on both the client and server sides to prevent attacks such as Cross-Site Scripting (XSS) and SQL Injection.

2. Cross-Site Scripting (XSS) Prevention:

- Use React's built-in mechanisms for rendering dynamic content safely, such as `dangerouslySetInnerHTML` and `react-dom`'s `escapeHTML`. Avoid rendering untrusted content directly in your components.

3. Cross-Site Request Forgery (CSRF) Protection:

- Implement anti-CSRF tokens to protect against Cross-Site Request Forgery attacks. Use libraries or frameworks that provide CSRF protection mechanisms.

4. Content Security Policy (CSP):

- Implement a Content Security Policy to restrict the sources from which your application can load scripts, styles, and other resources. This can help mitigate various types of attacks, including XSS.

5. Authentication and Authorization:

- Implement secure authentication mechanisms, such as JWT (JSON Web Tokens) or OAuth, to ensure that users are who they claim to be.

- Use role-based or attribute-based access control to determine whether users have permission to access specific resources or perform certain actions within your application.

6. Secure API Requests:

- When making API requests, use secure communication protocols (HTTPS) and include proper authentication and authorization headers. Avoid exposing sensitive data or API keys in your client-side code.

7. Secure Password Storage:

- If your application handles user authentication, store passwords securely using strong, salted, and hashed password storage mechanisms. Avoid storing plain text passwords.

8. Proper Error Handling:

- Implement proper error handling in your application. Avoid displaying detailed error messages to end-users that could reveal sensitive information. Log errors securely on the server.

9. Avoid Hardcoding Secrets:

- Avoid hardcoding secrets (e.g., API keys, database credentials) directly in your code. Use environment variables or secret management tools to securely manage and access sensitive information.

10. Regular Security Audits:

- Conduct regular security audits and vulnerability assessments of your React application. Use security scanning tools and follow best practices for identifying and fixing security issues.

11. Keep Dependencies Updated:

- Regularly update your project's dependencies, including React itself, to ensure you are using the latest, most secure versions. Vulnerabilities in dependencies can affect your application's security.

12. Data Encryption:

- Encrypt sensitive data both in transit (using HTTPS) and at rest (using encryption mechanisms provided by your database or storage system).

13. Secure Cookies:

- When handling authentication cookies, ensure that they are marked as "Secure" and "HttpOnly" to protect against certain attacks, such as session hijacking and XSS.

14. Security Education:

- Train your development team on secure coding practices and security best practices. Security awareness is crucial for preventing vulnerabilities.

15. Third-Party Libraries:

- Be cautious when using third-party libraries and components. Ensure that they are well-maintained and do not introduce security vulnerabilities.

16. Disaster Recovery and Incident Response:

- Have a plan in place for handling security incidents and data breaches. Implement disaster recovery measures to minimize the impact of security incidents.

By implementing these security considerations in your React applications, you can reduce the risk of security vulnerabilities and ensure that your application remains secure and protected against common threats. Security should be an ongoing process, with continuous monitoring and improvement to address emerging threats and vulnerabilities.

Keeping Up with React

React continuously evolves with new features, updates, and best practices, so staying up-to-date is crucial for React developers. Here are some strategies for keeping up with React:

1. Official React Documentation:

- Start with the official React documentation (https://react.dev/). It's the most reliable and comprehensive resource for learning React and staying informed about the latest updates.

2. React Blog and Release Notes:

- Subscribe to the React blog (https://react.dev/blog) and regularly review the release notes. The React team provides detailed information about new features, improvements, and breaking changes.

3. Community Forums and Newsletters:

- Join React-related forums like the Reactiflux Discord community and the Reactiflux GitHub repository. These platforms are great for discussions, asking questions, and sharing knowledge.

- Subscribe to newsletters like "React Status" (https://react.statuscode.com/) to receive regular updates, articles, and news about the React ecosystem.

4. Online Courses and Tutorials:

- Enroll in online courses and tutorials on platforms like Udemy, Coursera, and Pluralsight. Many instructors offer React courses that cover the latest concepts and best practices.

5. Open Source Projects:

- Contribute to or follow open source React projects on GitHub. This is an excellent way to gain practical experience and learn from other developers.

6. Attend Conferences and Meetups:

- Attend React conferences, meetups, and webinars to network with other developers and hear from experts in the field. Popular events include ReactConf and local React meetups.

7. Follow Influential Developers:

- Follow influential React developers and experts on social media platforms like Twitter and LinkedIn. They often share valuable insights, code snippets, and links to useful resources.

8. Read React-related Books:

- Invest in books on React, Redux, and related topics. Books provide in-depth knowledge and can be a valuable reference for advanced concepts.

9. Experiment and Build Projects:

- The best way to learn is by doing. Create your own React projects, experiment with new features, and apply best practices. Practical experience is invaluable.

10. Stay Updated on Related Technologies:

- React often integrates with other technologies and libraries (e.g., Redux, React Router). Stay informed about updates and best practices for these related technologies.

React is a dynamic and rapidly evolving ecosystem, so continuous learning is essential for staying relevant as a React developer. By following these strategies, you can keep up with the latest developments, best practices, and trends in the React community and ensure that your React skills remain up-to-date and marketable.

Appendices

<u>Glossary</u>

In the Appendices section of your book, including a glossary can be a valuable resource for readers. It provides clear definitions and explanations for key terms and concepts related to React and web development. Here's a sample glossary you can include:

1. React:
   - React is an open-source JavaScript library for building user interfaces. It allows developers to create reusable UI components and manage the state of an application efficiently.

2. Component:
   - In React, a component is a reusable piece of user interface that can contain HTML, CSS, and JavaScript. Components can be composed to build complex user interfaces.

3. JSX (JavaScript XML):
   - JSX is a syntax extension for JavaScript used in React to define the structure of UI components. It resembles HTML but is transpiled into JavaScript.

4. Virtual DOM (VDOM):
   - The Virtual DOM is a concept in React where a virtual representation of the actual DOM is created. It allows React to update the real DOM efficiently by comparing changes in the virtual representation.

5. Props (Properties):
   - Props are used to pass data from parent to child components in React. They are read-only and help make components reusable and configurable.

6. State:
  - State represents the data that a component can maintain and change over time. When state changes, React re-renders the component to reflect the updated data.

7. Lifecycle Methods:
  - Lifecycle methods are special methods in React components that allow you to perform actions at specific points in a component's lifecycle, such as when it's mounted or updated.

8. Redux:
  - Redux is a state management library for React applications. It helps manage the global state of an application in a predictable and consistent way.

9. Router:
  - In React, a router is used to handle navigation and routing within a single-page application. React Router is a popular library for managing routing in React applications.

10. DOM (Document Object Model):
  - The DOM is a programming interface for web documents. It represents the structure of an HTML document and allows scripts to access and manipulate the document's content.

11. API (Application Programming Interface):
  - An API is a set of rules and protocols that allows one software application to interact with another. In the context of web development, APIs are often used to fetch data from servers.

12. SPA (Single-Page Application):
  - A SPA is a web application that loads a single HTML page and dynamically updates its content as the user interacts with the application. React is often used to build SPAs.

13. Component State vs. Redux State:
  - Explains the difference between local component state and global state managed by Redux.

14. Prop Drilling:
   - Prop drilling occurs when data needs to be passed through multiple levels of nested components, which can be inefficient. It's a common challenge in React.

15. Hooks:
   - React Hooks are functions that let you use state and other React features in functional components. They were introduced in React 16.8.

16. JSX Elements:
   - JSX elements are the building blocks of React components. They describe what should be rendered on the screen and can include HTML-like tags.

17. Babel:
   - Babel is a JavaScript compiler that allows you to use the latest JavaScript features in your code by transpiling it to an older version of JavaScript that's compatible with most browsers.

18. Webpack:
   - Webpack is a popular JavaScript module bundler used to bundle and optimize assets like JavaScript, CSS, and images for web applications.

19. NPM (Node Package Manager):
   - NPM is a package manager for JavaScript that allows developers to install and manage packages and dependencies for their projects.

20. CDN (Content Delivery Network):
   - A CDN is a network of geographically distributed servers that deliver web content, including static assets like CSS and JavaScript, to users faster and more efficiently.

21. SPA (Single-Page Application):
   - A SPA is a web application that loads a single HTML page and dynamically updates its content as the user interacts with the application. React is often used to build SPAs.

22. SSR (Server-Side Rendering):

- SSR is a technique in which web pages are initially rendered on the server before being sent to the client. It can improve SEO and initial page load performance.

23. CSR (Client-Side Rendering):
- CSR is a technique in which web pages are initially rendered on the client's browser using JavaScript. It provides a more interactive user experience.

24. Redux Thunk:
- Redux Thunk is a middleware for Redux that allows you to write asynchronous logic (such as API calls) in Redux actions.

25. Redux Saga:
- Redux Saga is a middleware for Redux that provides a more advanced way to handle asynchronous operations and side effects.

26. Higher-Order Component (HOC):
- A HOC is a design pattern in React that allows you to reuse component logic by wrapping one component with another. It's often used for cross-cutting concerns like authentication.

27. JSX Spread Attributes:
- JSX spread attributes allow you to pass all the properties of an object as props to a component. This can make your code more concise and maintainable.

28. CSS Modules:
- CSS Modules are a way to locally scope CSS styles to a component, preventing style conflicts in larger applications.

29. Styled Components:
- Styled Components is a library that allows you to write CSS-in-JS by defining component-specific styles directly in your JavaScript code.

30. Prop Types:
- Prop Types is a library that provides runtime type checking for the props passed to React components. It helps catch and diagnose errors early.

31. Render Prop:
   - A render prop is a technique where a component's render method is passed as a function prop to another component. It's used for sharing code between components.

32. PureComponent:
   - PureComponent is a class component in React that performs a shallow comparison of props and state to determine if a re-render is necessary. It can improve performance.

33. Code Splitting:
   - Code splitting is a technique that involves breaking a large bundle of JavaScript into smaller chunks that are loaded only when needed. It improves initial page load times.

34. Lazy Loading:
   - Lazy loading is a technique where assets (such as images or components) are loaded asynchronously when they are needed, reducing initial load times.

35. Progressive Web App (PWA):
   - A PWA is a web application that provides a native app-like experience, including offline access, push notifications, and fast performance.

36. GraphQL:
   - GraphQL is a query language for APIs that allows clients to request exactly the data they need. It provides more flexibility and efficiency compared to traditional REST APIs.

37. Web Accessibility (a11y):
   - Web accessibility refers to the practice of making web content and applications usable by people with disabilities. It includes considerations for screen readers and keyboard navigation.

38. CORS (Cross-Origin Resource Sharing):

- CORS is a security feature implemented by web browsers that controls which domains are allowed to make requests to a web application. It helps prevent cross-site request forgery.

39. Babel Presets and Plugins:
   - Babel presets and plugins are configurations and extensions used with the Babel compiler to enable specific JavaScript features or transformations.

40. Ecosystem:
   - In the context of React, the ecosystem refers to the collection of libraries, tools, and technologies that work together with React to build web applications.

These terms cover a range of topics related to React and web development, helping readers gain a more comprehensive understanding of the terminology and concepts used in your book.

Index